Gardening Indoors with Rockwool

by George F. Van Patten
Alyssa F. Bust

Published by Van Patten Publishing
Cover Design: Dennis Stovall, Blue Heron Publishing
Artwork: Hart James
Book Design: G. F. Van Patten
Cover Photo: Courtesy Agro Dynamics, Inc. Ventura, CA.
The model is Vibeke Kjoeljede. Thanks Vibeke!
Back Cover Photos: Courtesy Agro Dynamics, Inc. Ventura, CA.
Copyright 1997, George F. Van Patten
ISBN 1-878823-22-1
First Printing
9 8 7 6 5 4 3 2 1

This book is written for the purpose of supplying gardening information to the public. It is sold with the agreement that it does not offer any guarantee of plant growth or well-being. Readers of this book are responsible for all plants cultivated. You are encouraged to read any and all information available about indoor gardening and gardening in general to develop a complete background on the subjects so you can tailor this information to your individual needs. This book should be used as a general guide to gardening indoors and not the ultimate source.

The authors and Van Patten Publishing have tried to the best of their abilities to describe all of the most current methods used to garden successfully indoors. However, there may be some mistakes in the text that the authors and publisher were unable to detect. This book contains current information up to the date of publication.

Neither the publisher nor the authors endorse any products or brand names that are mentioned or pictured in the text. Products are pictured or mentioned for illustration only.

We, the authors, want to extend a big "Thank You" to all the expert editors that edited this book!

Australia - Doug Drummond, Vivien Ireland, Robin Moseby, Gramme Plummer,

Canada -Ron Hayes, Wayne Hayes, Andre Courte, Guy Dionne, Tom Duncan, Jim Gower, Scott Hammond, Sharon Harper, Keith Harper, R. Markiewicz, Frank Pastor, Russ Rea, Shelley Rea, Don Stewart, William Sutherland, Francois Wolf Jr.

New Zealand - Rob Smith

UK - Giles Gunstone

USA - Tom Alexander, Carl Anderson, Bolt, Larry Brooke, John Bucher, Gordon Carter, Michael Christian, Mosen Daha, Bill Dalzell, Will Dalzell, Peter DePaola, Vince Dinapoli, Dr. Dioxide, Bob Edberg, Jeff Edwards, Bill Fetner Jr., Jeff Gibson, Kim Hanna, Tina Havro, Martin Heydt, Jim Howell, Christine Hubbard, David Ittel, Darryl Johnston, Ron Kleinman, Rick Martin, Tiffany Martin, Richard Middlebrook, Richard Miller, Tracy Peltzer, John Pierce, Nancy Pierce, Waymon Price, Brandy Price, Rajaim Purcifel, Chris Rothe, Chris Schneider, Tom Shelsky, Steve Stragnola, Brooke Taggert, Roger Thayer, Richey Truce, Larisa Ullrich, Jerry Van Volkenburg, Patrick Vivian

Special thanks to Dan Lubkeman, who added the finishing touches to this work.

Plant a row for the hungry!

This book is dedicated to the Plant a Row for the Hungry Program. This wonderful program has been growing rapidly across America and we would like to see it grow worldwide. The premise is simple, plant one extra row or bed in your garden and give it to hungry people.

Your local telephone book has the names of several agencies, such as Second Harvest, that will help you distribute your bounty.

Plant a Row for the Hungry!

Table of Contents

Chapter One
An Introduction to Rockwool

Indoor Gardening

Until relatively recently, hobby and professional gardeners both assumed losses during winter months. Although gardeners can control many aspects of a plant's environment (water, fertilizer, growing medium), they can not control the cycle of the sun. In most regions of the United States, the reduction of light intensity during winter months has been a prohibitive factor for gardeners. Not only are days shorter in the winter, but the sun's light is also less intense due to its position in the sky and an increase in cloud coverage. In the past, gardeners resigned themselves to a short growing season and gardened only during the sun's peak seasons.

Now, however, with the development of indoor lighting technology, gardeners can control the amount of light their plants receive year-round. The pleasures and benefits of gardening are no longer controlled by seasons. Instead, because indoor gardening provides gardeners with control and flexibility, gardeners can successfully grow plants without being limited by seasons, space, and uncontrollable weather.

Professional gardeners can enjoy profits year round. In addition, they can control their plants' growth cycles to plan crops according to market demands. The benefits are not limited to professionals. Hobbyists can enjoy fresh fruits, vegetables, and flowers from their gardens year-round.

Hydroponics

Many people associate hydroponic gardening primarily with space travel. Although NASA uses hydroponic gardening to feed astronauts, hydroponic gardens are as easy and successful on earth, in private homes, as they are in space and research labs. When you garden indoors, whether you are a professional or a hobbyist, you assume the responsibilities of Mother Nature. To ensure a healthy, productive garden, you must provide optimum light, water, fertilizer, humidity, heat, nutrients, and growing medium. Many gardeners have found it is easiest to control these factors while growing hydroponically. Hydroponic gardening is a method of growing plants without soil.

The benefits of gardening hydroponically are numerous. Successful gardeners have found that hydroponic plants grow faster, yield more, and cost less than those plants grown in soil.. In addition, many gardeners who struggled to keep soil-grown plants alive, are able to maintain healthy and productive hydroponic gardens. By using grow lights, gardeners can provide adequate light for photosynthesis all year, thereby extending their growing season, profit, and pleasure. By using a soilless growing material, gardeners gain optimum control over their plants' environment and avoid some of the obstacles associated with soil-based gardens. With hydroponic gardens, soilborne fungi, nematodes and weeds are minimal because soilless mixtures are free of disease organisms, insects, and weed seeds. However contamination is possible. Pathogenic fungi multiply rapidly due to the lack of competition for food and space. Because hydroponically-produced plants are grown in an inert material, the gardener has complete control over the nutrient content of the growing medium. Some hydroponic systems use no growing medium besides water. The plant roots are suspended in a chamber and are misted with liquid nutrients.

In addition, hydroponic gardens are ideal when space is limited. Because nutrients and water are delivered directly to the plants, you can direct more of the plants' energy in vegetative and flowering processes. Nutrients are dissolved in water, and are therefore immediately available to the plants' roots. Because the plants do not have to search for food, they spend more time growing, thus shortening the duration between seed and harvest. Root competition, however, is not eliminated and adequate space must be allowed for plenty of root mass. Being able to maximize space is a great benefit to professionals and hobbyists alike. For production growers, maximizing space equates to maximizing profits. In fact, one study which compared the per-acre yields of hydroponic and soil-based gardens reported increases of 420 to 1,800 percent for certain crops in hydroponic gardens.

For the hobby grower with little space, hydroponics provides the opportunity to produce a viable garden. Gardens can be established in as little space as a windowsill. In addition, soilless mixtures are light weight, making them an ideal option for hanging plants. For apartment dwellers who do not have much space and who do not enjoy hauling heavy soil up numerous flights of stairs, hydroponic gardens offer an attractive alternative. In addition, hydroponic gardeners avoid the mess which working with soil often creates.

Creating a hydroponic garden does not require a huge investment. Although many gardeners enjoy working in a greenhouse, one is by no means necessary for a successful garden. In fact, a corner of your basement, a section of your garage, a large closet, or even a sunny windowsill can be used as productive garden space.

Several kinds of soilless growing media are available on the market, including perlite, vermiculite, expanded clay or geolite, and rockwool. In this book we focus on rockwool because gardeners have found it to be a productive, cost-effective medium in which to grow hydroponically. In the following chapters you will find a discussion about the basic tenants of using rockwool in hydroponic gardening. In addition, this book provides detailed information about how to set up and maintain a rockwool garden.

Rockwool

Rockwool or stonewool is one of several soilless media available to gardeners today. This sterile material made from molten rock is the greatest innovation in growing media since sterilized soil.

Horticultural rockwool is made from a combination of molten (1600 degrees C) basalt rock, limestone and coke. The thin fibers are coated with a binding agent and cured in a large oven. After the curing process, the material is cut into various shapes to produce slabs, blocks, cubes or flock.

Rockwool gardens can be created from rockwool cubes, rockwool slabs, or rockwool flock. Rockwool cubes can be purchased in different sizes to meet different garden needs. Cube gardens are ideal for plant propagation and growing small plants, while slab gardens work well for larger plants and transplants. Rockwool flock, also known as granulated rockwool, is used primarily as an amendment to other growing media, or for single potted house plants.

A Brief History

Rockwool is a relatively new gardening innovation, rockwool-like substances have been made by natural forces for centuries. When volcanoes erupt, tiny droplets of molten lava are sprayed into the air. In Hawaii, where humans first noted the natural process of making "rockwool", tropical winds whip this magma into long, thin, hair-like fibers. These fibers are known in Hawaii as "Pele's hair", Pele being the Hawaiian God of volcanoes. For centuries this volcanic product has been collected and used to cultivate orchids and other plants.

Humans learned from nature and began producing rockwool. By 1865, it was produced in the United States and used as insulation. More than a hundred years later in Denmark, rockwool was developed for horticultural purposes. Like perlite, vermiculite, and numerous other soilless mixes, rockwool was first used by commercial growers. When European production growers became dissatisfied with their growing medium options, they searched for alternatives. Inorganic media such as sand, gravel, and perlite do not hold as much nutrient solution as does rockwool. In addition, sterilizing these inorganic materials is expensive. Because of these considerations, European growers were prompted to explore alternative growing media. Danish growers began using rockwool in their hydroponic gardens in the early 1970s.

Rockwool was such a success in European communities, that now essentially all cucumbers in Denmark are grown in rockwool. In 1984 in Holland, land under cultivation in

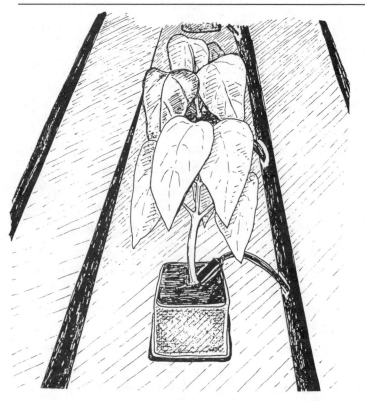

Strong cucumber crop in rockwool slabs.

rockwool doubled from 2,500 to 5,000 acres. In fact, today more than fifty percent of all Western European greenhouse vegetables are grown exclusively in rockwool.

As rockwool became popular in Europe, it also became an acceptable alternative in Asian countries. Japan began producing horticultural rockwool in 1984. Since then, many Japanese growers have started to switch to rockwool because they have found that it offers them the best value of any growing medium. In particular, the Japanese use rockwool extensively to propagate rice.

It was not until 1985 that horticultural rockwool was introduced into the United States and Canada. Rockwool caught on fast in Canada's progressive greenhouse industry. Greenhouse vegetable growers in Ontario and British Columbia, Canada use more and more rockwool in their gardens each year. Rockwool has been slower to gain popularity with commercial growers in the United States. Because the United States still possess many acres of fertile land, it is difficult for American growers to abandon soil-based agriculture. In the United States, rockwool is slowly gaining prominence among indoor gardeners, professionals and hobbyists alike. Tomatoes, cucumbers, peppers, lettuce, roses, freesias, and orchids are some crops now commonly grown in rockwool in the US.

How Rockwool Is Made

In order to understand some of rockwool's unique qualities, it is important to first understand where rockwool comes from and how it is made. Rockwool is made from thin fibers of a combination of volcanic rock, limestone, and coke. Human-made rockwool is produced in a similar manner as is its natural counterpart. The rigid rock components are melted at temperatures between 1400 - 1600 degrees Celsius. The molten solution is then poured in a spinning drum. As the molten solution flies out of the drum, it elongates and cools to form hair-like fibers. See photo of spinning drums on the back cover.

After the spinning process, a binder (phenol-based resin) is added to the rockwool fibers. This plastic-like binder prevents potassium hydroxide and other elements from leaching into the nutrient solution. After the binder is added, the rockwool is pressed and cured into large uniform slabs. The amount of pressure applied when forming the slabs dictates the density of the rockwool. Once formed, the slabs are rigid and easy to handle. They may be cut into many sizes and shapes. Most cubes are wrapped in a plastic sleeve with open ends. Rockwool flock usually comes in three grades: coarse, medium and fine. The flock may be either water repellent (like the insulation that it is designed after), or water absorbent. Granulated rockwool flock is easily placed into growing containers or used like vermiculite, perlite, or peat moss as a soil additive.

The direction in which the rockwool fibers run is important to water absorption. Nearly all slabs sold in North America have vertical fibers. The vertical fibers slabs hold up much better when reused. Horizontal grain slabs have a low compressive strength and tend to drain poorly. Small cubes have a vertical grain. The vertical grained cubes are perfect for the more rapid draining required by seedlings and clones. In addition, these vertical fibers stimulate downward root growth in seedlings and cuttings. Rockwool flock, promotes root growth in all directions because of the random orientation it its fibers.

The heat used to produce rockwool renders it sterile and safe for growing plants. The length and thickness of the rockwool fibers are regulated by the speed of the spinning drum, the consistency of the molten mix, and the melting temperature. The end-product is a very consistent rockwool, which contains little shot (mineral pellets that have not been spun into fiber, characteristic of insulation or low-grade rock-wool).

Several manufactures produce rockwool. However, foreign manufactures typically offer more complete product lines than do their American competitors.

Grodan is one of the most popular brands of rock-wool. Grodan is now made in Ontario, Canada and Denmark.

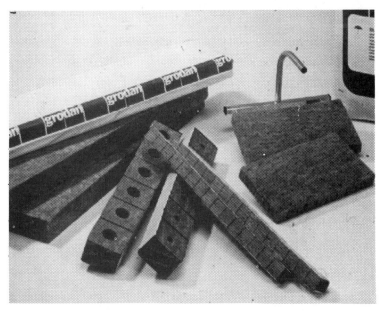

Rockwool is available in slabs, cubes and granular flock.

Many gardeners choose it because of excellent quality, availability and economical price. Other brands include Capogro from Great Britain (Grodan), Cultilene, French-made rockwool, Basala (Grodan) rockwool manufactured in Holland, Partek rockwool from Finland. Rockwool is also manufactured in Korea and Australia. Growool, manufactured in Australia, is very popular there. Ask for advice on selecting rockwool at your local gardening or hydroponic supply store.

Grades of Rockwool

Rockwool is not used exclusively for gardening. In fact, rockwool was first manufactured as insulation. Insulation grade rockwool can be used as a soil amendment but is not ideal for hydroponics. Because the water absorbent type retains moisture and facilitates drainage, it can be used to line hanging baskets containing annual or perennial plants. For most gardening purposes, however, it is important to buy horticultural grade rockwool. Although it is more expensive, the horticultural grade is preferable to insulation grade for indoor gardening.

Rockwool used for insulation is similar to that used for horticulture. However, it is the wrong density and does not contain a wetting agent. Horticultural rockwool is produced from basalt rock and is usually a combination of rock, limestone, and coke. The best horticultural rockwool is produced from volcanic basaltic rock. These rockwools have a mineral balance that is inert and will not react adversely with nutrient solution. High quality horticultural rockwool has uniform fibers, even distribution of the binder, and virtually no shot. This high quality rockwool weighs less than five pounds per cubic foot.

 Rule of Thumb: Use horticultural grade rockwool for best results.

Some insulation grade rockwool, on the other hand, is produced from steel or copper slag, a waste product from smelting. These rockwools contain a high amount of metals, mainly copper and iron, that may react with nutrient solution. Low quality insulation grade rockwool also contains more problem-causing shot, and weighs seven pounds or more per cubic foot. Insulation grade rockwool compacts relatively easily. Although still porous and well-draining, this compaction upsets the air-water ratio that is so important to all hydroponic growing media. The other problem with insulation grade rockwool is pH drift. pH drift is caused by substances, primarily calcium carbonate from the limestone, being released

A magnified cross section of rockwool.

into the nutrient solution and raising the pH. The weathering of basalt potassium hydroxide naturally causes the pH to drift above seven, and in extreme cases, to as high as ten. A high pH level locks out many elements that plants need to absorb from the nutrient solution. The binder also causes water repulsion.

NOTE: Uniform wetting is one of horticultural rockwool's most important qualities. It promotes even root growth, and provides even drainage. Remember, all wetting agents wash out after 3-4 months.

The Rockwool Comparison

Like all growing media, rockwool has both advantages and disadvantages. But after experimenting with both, many gardeners prefer soilless rooting media to soil mixtures. Rockwool, in particular, offers some advantages over both soil mixtures and other soilless media. Not only are organic growing media like peat, sawdust, and soils becoming more expensive to produce, but they also possess several critical drawbacks. With time, they decompose and experience changes in their water holding capacity. Other inorganic media such as sand, gravel, and perlite neither hold as much nutrient solution nor offer as much buffering capacity as does rockwool.

Rockwool's biggest advantage is an effect of its construction. Between ninety and ninety-five percent of the space between rockwool's fibers is filled with air, and it holds more nutrient solution and air than any other growing medium. This air space makes oxygen, water, and nutrient solution easily accessible to plant roots.

Rockwool is also easy to handle and easy to use. It is available in a variety of sizes and shapes. Rockwool can be purchased in many garden stores, particularly those that sell hydroponic equipment. Using this dry material eliminates much of the mess of gardening. There is no heavy soil to lug around or clean up. For the sometimes gardener who wants the benefit of plants, but does not want the commitment of a serious garden, rockwool flock is ideal. Some house plants such as cactus grown in rockwool flock only need to be watered once a month. For people who enjoy travelling a lot, this added flexibility can be the deciding factor between no garden and a successful garden.

In addition to being easy to handle, rockwool is easy to control. It is sterile and consistent. There is no guessing game as there may be when you are preparing a soil mixture. High quality rockwool neither reacts to nor changes the nutrient balance or mineral composition of the applied solution.

Rockwool is particularly well suited to propagation. The downward fibers of rockwool cubes encourage downward root growth in young seedlings and clones. Some rockwool cubes come attached in a sheet which fits neatly into a propagation tray. You can purchase pre-punched rockwool with holes for either seedling transplants or cuttings. In addition, it is easy to tell when clones have rooted. You can often see the roots pop out the bottom of the cube. Rockwool also makes transplanting effortless. Rockwool cubes are simply transplanted into larger pots. You do not need to worry about separating and potentially damaging the frail root system from its growing medium.

Rockwool is also a cost-effective choice. In fact, one-inch rockwool cubes generally retail for half the cost of peat pellets. Although rockwool is often initially more expensive than soil (it can be up to ten times as expensive to root an equal amount of cuttings), it is a better value than other media because with care and sterilization, it can last indefinitely. In between uses, remove any old root systems and sterilize the medium. Try to remove at least ninety to ninety-five percent of the roots to avoid potential clogs which prohibit effective draining. Gardeners use steam or bleach to sterilize the rockwool . Mix one cup of bleach in five gallons of water and flood the rockwool for at least an hour. Then spend at least an hour flushing the sterilizing solution out of the medium (and any equipment you sterilized) with clean water. Turn the slabs over, with the bottom side up, to reuse with best results.

Because of rockwool's unique qualities, a successful rockwool garden can easily yield between ten and twenty percent more produce than a comparable soil garden. This yield increase can be raised to approximately fifty percent if a few simple cultivation techniques are employed.

Although the advantages out-weigh the disadvantages, rockwool does possess some detriments of which gardeners

should be aware. When dry, rockwool can irritate your skin.
Like peat moss, dry rockwool acts as an abrasive. Wear
gloves, goggles, and a face mask or respirator when working
with dry rockwool. Because wet rockwool does not create
dust or irritate the skin, many gardeners wet it slightly before
handling. Misting the air when breaking up a large bail of dry
flock will keep dust to a minimum. Keep dry rockwool out of
the reach of children and pets. As an additional safety precau-
tion, wash your clothes after working with rockwool.

Although it is important to handle dry rockwool with
care, the physical characteristics of rockwool are different
from those of other dangerous materials, such as asbestos.
Rockwool fibers consist of single monofilament strands which
are bunched together. These fibers will not split lengthwise to
form thinner fibrils. Asbestos fibers, on the other hand, split
lengthwise into ultra-thin fibrils that penetrate the body and
its cell walls. The body has difficulty passing them or breaking them down. Rockwool fibers, however, are much thicker
and break across the length to yield a short, fat fiber that the
body can easily discharge and dissolve.

Because rockwool stays so moist, algae see it as an
inviting home. While green algae is unsightly, the algae itself
is not a problem for your plants because it does not compete
with the plant for nutrients. However, if the algae turns black
and slimy (decaying) it can harbor bacteria or viruses that can
affect your plants. The algae can also attract fungus gnats.
Dead, decaying algae can also rob your plants of oxygen necessary for nutrient uptake. To avoid an algae problem, simply
cover your rockwool with opaque plastic to exclude light.
Algae needs light to grow. If the problem persists, you can use
yellow sticky traps to catch unwanted fungus gnats. Seven
(Carbaryl) will kill larvae. A thin layer of gravel, expanded
clay or leca over the rockwool will also help discourage the

Wear long sleeves, gloves and a mask when breaking up dry rockwool.

growth of fungus gnats.

For cuttings, the algae growth will not be as much of a problem before they root as it might be after. Before rooting, your cuttings should be partially shaded anyway. There are also several algaecides that can be added to the nutrient solution to control algae. Chemical algaecides are not recommended for use with food crops. If you decide to use an algaecide, read the label carefully to ensure it is not toxic to plants or people, and use it very sparingly.

Be selective with crops you grow hydroponically. A rockwool garden will not perform like a soil garden. Some

A young pepper plant growing in a cube.

crops such as root crops, trees, and vines are better suited to soil. For instance, potatoes, horseradish, asparagus, and fruit trees all grow better in traditional soil-based gardens.

For the most part, however, plants will thrive in rockwool gardens provided that you establish an efficient hydroponic system, control your garden environment, and feed your plants with a balanced nutrient solution. In the following chapters, you will learn how to establish and maintain a high-performance rockwool garden. The first step in gardening with rockwool is purchasing or making a hydroponic system. In the next chapter you will find a detailed discussion which will help you to do just that.

Chapter Two
A Hydroponic System

Rockwool gardens, though they can be established anywhere, do thrive in systems which require some basic equipment. It is not difficult or expensive to set up a hydroponic garden. You can purchase manufactured systems from many garden supply stores. It is also quite easy to establish your own. Depending on how automated your system is, you will need some or all of the following items: a reservoir, a garden bed, a pump, a timer, a heater, and a thermometer. None of these items require a huge investment, and all of them can be purchased at your local hardware or garden supply store. With the proper equipment and knowledge, you will be able to create a high-performance rockwool garden.

The first choice you need to make is between a circulating (also known as recirculating or active) and non-circulating (also know as non-recovery or passive) system. Hydroponic systems are classified by the way in which they deliver nutrient solution to the root zone. Non-circulating systems rely on capillary action for the nutrients to travel to the plants from a reservoir below. These passive systems work similar to the way a kerosene lamp works. In a kerosene lamp, fuel is wicked up from a basin to the flame. In a passive rockwool garden, nutrient solution is wicked from a reservoir to the garden bed where it is used by plants.

Because non-circulating systems do not require any mechanical parts, they are inexpensive to establish and maintain. With no moving parts, there is less of a chance for the systems to break or malfunction. In addition to being inexpensive, passive systems tend to require little maintenance. Once the system is established, it does not require much time or money.

NOTE: When nutrient solution is not recovered, complications and labor may be reduced, but the environment may suffer. This is true especially for commercial greenhouse growers who may dump large amounts of nutrients on the ground. These nutrients, both organic and chemical,   ultimately seep into the ground water and may damage both plant and animal life.

Most gardeners today, professional and hobbyist, rely on an active, or recirculating system. They conserve water and the environment and are more exact. In addition, as the solution is pumped and circulated, it collects oxygen. The more oxygen available to plants, the healthier they will be. An active system does exactly what its name suggests— it actively circulates, and recirculates, the nutrient solution to the root zone. There are several different types of circulating systems on the market today. Although it is possible to make your own active system out of household supplies, most models require mechanical equipment. For instance, most active systems employ a pump and tubing to deliver the liquid to the plants and then collect the runoff for redistribution.
In the following chapter you will find a detailed discussion of

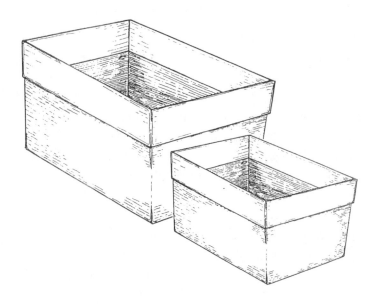

The reservoir on the left is 50% larger than the one on the right. The larger reservoir is much more practical for a hydroponic garden.

the equipment needed to establish either a circulating or a non-circulating system. If you choose a passive system, you will need little more than a reservoir, a garden bed, and a wicking method. If you want to employ an active system, you will also need to consider pumps, filters, and timers.

Reservoirs

The reservoir and the garden bed work together to form the two fundamental elements of both circulating and non-circulating systems. The reservoir serves as a temporary storage bin for the nutrient solution. Although there are differences in the way in which reservoirs function in circulating and non-circulating systems, there are some basic guidelines to follow when creating a reservoir. The larger the reservoir the better. Think of your reservoir as a buffering system which guards against short term changes in nutrient concentrations and pH levels. In order to compensate for evaporation and transpiration, a reservoir should hold at least 25 to 50 percent more nutrient solution than it takes to fill the garden beds or irrigate the rockwool. Gardens that hold larger amounts of nutrient solution tend to be more forgiving and easier to control.

A reservoir can be any size or shape as long as it holds water and does not react to chemicals. Plastic storage bins, plastic trash cans, Rubbermaid trays, large wooden bins lined with 20 mil plastic (water bed liner), or even old bath tubs can all make excellent reservoirs. A large galvanized livestock water trough will hold hundreds of gallons of nutrient solution. If you use a galvanized troughs, line it with heavy (10 to 20 mil) plastic. A children's swimming pool holds large volumes of nutrient solution and can be used as a cost-effective reservoir. Commercial greenhouses use concrete pits coated with inert paint as reservoirs. These pits are typically located underneath greenhouses.

Anticipate a water loss of 5 to 25 percent daily, depending on climatic conditions and plant size. For example, a fast growing vegetable garden with a 30 gallon reservoir uses between 3 and 9 gallons of solution a day. Three consecutive hot days can cause the reservoir to run dry. Water evaporation is a problem not only because it robs plants of moisture, but also because as the water level reduces, the concentration of nutrients increases. Because nutrients do not evaporate when water does, they become concentrated to unacceptable levels.

New nutrient solution added into a reservoir full of imbalanced nutrient can severely limit plant growth.

To reduce evaporation (and reduce algae), cover your rockwool with plastic and place a top on the reservoir. A sophisticated garden will employ a float valve (see drawing) that adds water as it is used from the reservoir. In manual systems, a "full" line on the inside of the reservoir tank shows when the solution is low. Add water daily, or as soon as the solution level drops below the indicated line.

If water is not replenished as its level falls, the iron level can increase up to three fold, while the magnesium level can easily double. Other nutrient levels usually remain relatively constant. Refer to pH and Conductivity Factor (CF is the measure of the electrical conductivity of a solution) readings to measure overall change in the nutrient solution. Do not assume that the pH or CF will remain constant. Remember, in a recirculating garden, plants use nutrients each time the solution cycles through. As plants use nutri-

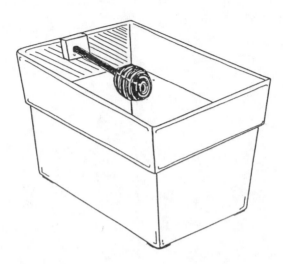

One of the many different types of float valves used to automatically fill a reservoir.

ents, the solution's concentration changes, thereby changing the pH level. In most cases, with each cycle the pH raises. Check your pH level daily and adjust it accordingly. One gardener reports that during heavy fruit and flower formation, the pH can actually drop. Another gardener reports that the pH will drop with potassium uptake.

Regardless of whether you use a non-circulating or circulating system, you will need to dispose of your spent nutrient solution. Although large reservoirs tend to be easier to control, it is less laborious to dispose of spent solution from a small reservoir. Whereas the depleted nutrient solution must be drained or pumped from a large reservoir, small reservoirs are easy to pick up and empty in the outdoor garden.

 Rule of Thumb: Check your pH level daily and adjust it accordingly.

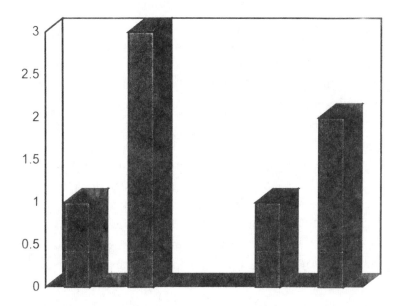

The iron level can climb three times as high and the magnesium level can double when replenished nutrients are out of balance.

To remove spent nutrient solution from a large reservoir, attach a hose to a pump and pump the depleted nutrient solution out of the reservoir. Do not drain depleted nutrients into a septic tank. Nitrates and other nutrients disrupt the chemistry of the septic tank and cause it to back up and overflow. Use the depleted nutrient solution in your outdoor garden. It also works well as a foliar spray outdoors.

If you are unable to pump the depleted nutrient solution out of the reservoir, siphon it out. Be careful; a mouthful of solution is unpleasant. To start the siphon, submerge the entire hose so that it fills with water. Put your thumb over one end of the hose to form an air lock. Remove the covered end of the hose and place it below the level of the reservoir. The hose, full of nutrient solution, will begin to siphon when you remove your thumb. Remember, a siphon only works when the outlet is below the input end.

Sludge on the bottom of the reservoir is generally inert and will not react with the new fertilizer, none-the-less clean it out. Attach a pump basket or a plastic kitchen scouring pad around the pump to filter out large debris. Use a turkey baster to pick up any solution left by the pump. A sponge will absorb the last bit of solution.

Use the spent nutrient solution on your vegetable garden, flower bed, or lawn. Although it is too depleted for your rockwool garden, the spent solution still contains many beneficial nutrients. Do not dump the runoff in the same location repeatedly. It will build-up in the soil and cause toxic salt burn. In extreme cases the runoff may pollute ground water. Salt build-up can also be a problem in containerized plants. If a white residue appears on the slab or around drain holes, you have salt build-up. Unless you flush your containerized plants with fresh water monthly, you should not use depleted nutrient solution on them.

Garden Beds

The garden bed is, as its name suggests, the growing area of a hydroponic system. A garden bed can be made of a deep tray, a growing table, a bucket, or virtually any container that will hold your plants, the rockwool, and an adequate amount of nutrient solution. Be certain not to choose a garden bed that will potentially react with your plants. For instance, many metals corrode and harm plants in the process.

Place presoaked (conditioned) rockwool cubes or slabs in your garden bed, and you are ready to garden. The capillary holding action of the rockwool will keep water in the slab or cube. Yet most of the water will concentrate in the lower one to two inches of the rockwool. There is therefore little or no need to fill your garden bed with slabs more than three or four inches thick.

In a passive system, the garden bed can be any appropriate growing container which accommodates a wick from the reservoir below. For active systems, nutrient solution is transported to the garden bed via mechanical means. There are many varieties of recirculating systems, each of which employs a slightly different means of transporting the nutrient solution. When you choose a system, consider durability, ease of use, expense, and convenience.

To calculate the amount of nutrient solution the garden bed can hold when it is totally flooded:

multiply length x width x depth = cubic volume

For example a table that is 48 x 24 x 6 inches has a
  volume of 6,912 cubic inches.
One cubic foot is 12 x 12 x 12 inches =
1,728 cubic inches.
So 6,912/1,728 inches = 4 cubic feet.
There are 7.48 gallons in a cubic foot.
4 feet x 7.48 gallons = 30 gallons
+ 25 percent of 30 = 7.5 = 30 + 7.5 =
37.5 gallons of nutrient needed.

A more simple, fool-proof way to calculate the necessary reservoir capacity is to fill the garden bed with pre-wet rockwool, flood the table to the desired depth, then measure the runoff.

Once you have calculated how much solution your garden bed holds, you need to guard against potential overflows. Regardless of how careful your calculation, overflowing is always a possibility. The easiest way to ensure that the garden bed does not overflow is to install an overflow port. The nutrient solution floods the garden bed up to the port. The port then drains the excess nutrient solution back into the reservoir. Because each irrigation cycle floods a garden bed with approximately one to two inches of solution, the port should be large enough to accommodate this amount of water.

Typically, it takes between five and fifteen minutes for a garden bed to fill, and ten to twenty for it to drain. How often you flood your garden bed depends on how fast roots dry out, the temperature, the size and number of plants in the bed, and the desired growth rate. Evaporation and transpiration are accelerated if there is natural wind or a fan blowing. In such conditions, roots take up nutrients more rapidly and the bed will need to be filled more frequently.

If the drain clogs, your garden bed is likely to overflow and your plants will suffer. Look for stainless steel or plastic sink drains found at hardware stores. They are noncorrosive and will not damage plants. To prevent roots and debris from clogging the drain, place a nylon stocking or a small mesh (quarter-inch or less) screen made from a noncorrosive material, over the drain. The screen should be easy to remove and clean. A plastic kitchen scouring pad makes a great drain and overflow port filter.

Pumps

Pumps play an invaluable role in many rockwool gardens. In an active system, a pump transports fresh nutrient solution from the reservoir to the garden bed. In addition, for plants to receive fresh nutrients, it is essential that the spent solution be removed for the reservoir. For a system which is too large to lift, you may choose to employ a hose and a pump.

Before selecting a pump, it is important to understand the basic difference between several models of recirculating, active systems. In some hydroponic gardens, the nutrient solution is fed to the garden bed from the bottom, while in others it supplied from the top. The type of pump you need will depend on the type of system you establish. Some systems require submersible pumps, while others only require air pumps.

In one model of a top feed system, known as a drip emitter system, nutrient solution is transported to the rockwool via a pump and some tubing. The main tubing connects to smaller feeder tubes which deliver the nutrient solution to the base of plants. As opposed to flooding the entire bed, this system allows the nutrient solution to trickle into the rockwool and moisten it. Gravity then carries it back the the reservoir. Inexpensive submersible pumps are ideal for such hydroponic rockwool gardens.

In a different top feed model, lets call it the top feed air pump method, air is pumped into the reservoir through a small tube. This small tube is placed inside a larger tube which is connected to a "soaker" tube. This "soaker" tube is placed on the surface of the growing medium. The larger tube creates pressure and draws the solution up from the reservoir into the garden bed.

No tubing is needed in a bottom feed system. Instead, air is pumped directly into the reservoir. This creates pressure which forces nutrient solution from the reservoir into the growing bed.

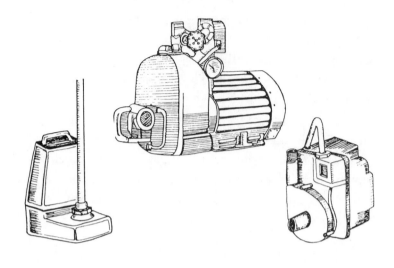

Several different hydroponic pumps. The two small pumps on the left are submersible. The large high-pressure pump on the right is not submersible.

Pumps are rated by their ability to perform several different functions. They are rated by the gallons per hour (GPH) they can move, the pounds per square inch (PSI) under which they can operate, and the maximum height or "head" they can lift a solution. If you know the maximum head a pump delivers, divide that figure by 2.31 to get the PSI of the pump. For example, a pump with a 6-foot head has a PSI rating of 2.6 (6 divided by 2.31 = 2.6). A pump with a head of 40 feet has a PSI rating of 17.32. City water is usually delivered at a pressure between 50 and 80 PSI. The GPH rating and the maximum head rating are also interrelated. Generally, the higher a pump has to lift the water (i.e. the larger the head), the less volume it can move. For example, a 275 GPH pump will lift 275 GPH one foot high in one hour, 225 GPH at a three-foot head, 200 GPH at a five-foot head and 25 GPH nine feet high.

To keep a pump from being overworked, use one that supplies 20 to 50 percent more capacity than you need. For example, to fill a 20-gallon garden bed in less than 10 minutes and lift it 3 feet from the bottom of a reservoir, use a submersible pump that delivers at least 150 GPH through a 1/2" hose.

To find the proper pump for your hydroponic garden use the following formula:

$$\frac{\text{Volume in gallons in the garden bed}}{\text{time to fill garden bed}} =$$

GPH x 60 minutes = GPH pump

To supply 20 gallons in 10 minutes and lift it 3 feet:

20 gallons/10 minutes = 2 gallons per minute

2 gallons per minute x 60 minutes = 120 GPH

Use a pump that delivers 120 GPH or more.

Height Lifted	1'	3'	5'	7'	9'
	120	70	40	-	-
GPH	170	130	70	-	-
of	205	170	120	40	-
pump	300	250	200	160	110
	500	350	280	200	150
	700	520	350	280	200

Various pumps delivering water over one foot high to drip emitters. This chart is approximate. Different brands of pumps will vary in their performance. Tubing size will also affect the GPH. The larger the tubing, the more GPH; the smaller the tubing, the less GPH.

| Pump 1.0 GPH | | 0.5 GPH | 0.3 GPH |
GPH	Emitter	Emitter	Emitter
40	20	35	40
70	35	70	120
120	50	100	150
150	70	150	200
170	80	170	300
200	90	200	300
250	120	300	400
350	150	400	600
500	200	600	800

Small pumps loose efficiency very quickly while high volume pumps continue to lift almost as much solution at various heights.

When you are purchasing a pump, be aware that there are advantages and disadvantages to all options. Small, inexpensive, low volume pumps loose pressure and volume rapidly. They are suited for fewer drip emitters. Because there is less pressure, the friction in the hose is much greater, giving less nutrient flow.

More expensive pumps are designed to handle corrosive, hot, and cold materials. Most metals corrode and release chemical elements as by-products. These undesirable chemical have the potential of killing your plants. If your pH is lower than five, metal parts on inexpensive pumps are likely to corrode and disturb plant health. Although galvanized screws on these small, inexpensive pumps are usually not problematic, copper and brass pipes, fittings, and parts are. A non-corrosive pump is well worth the investment, especially if your garden typically has a low pH level. Stainless steel is the safest metal to use in a hydroponic system. It will not corrode

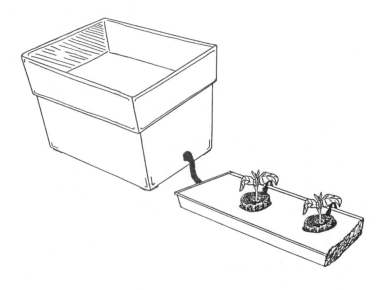

Watch for unwanted siphoning if your reservoir is located above emitters.

even when it comes in contact with an acidic nutrient solu-.
tion.

High pressure, high volume pumps are great for large gardens. Most of these high pressure pumps are not sub-mersible. They have a higher horsepower rating, and a rela-tively stable GPH capacity which does not deteriorate with height. For example, a high volume pump with a stronger motor, delivering 200 GPH could service 180 one-GPH emit-ters or 360 - 0.5 GPH drip emitters and still retain adequate pressure. These large, non-corrosive pumps can range in price from $200 to $800. If you buy a large pump, consult the supplier and study the specifications carefully.

Many submersible pump housings are cast aluminum covered with impermeable epoxy paint. The motor may be sealed in a non-electrical conducting oil. Be careful if you decide to open an oil bathed pump for internal inspection. The oil may leak out when the motor casing is removed. Some submersible pumps are not bathed in oil. These types of submersible pumps may overheat and burn if operated while not submerged. Check the pump's instructions to find a pump that shuts off when out of water or use a shut-off type float valve.

Submersible pumps only work when fully submerged in liquid. To prevent air locks, be certain that your garden is designed to keep the pump fully submerged at all times. Also, watch for unwanted siphoning if your reservoir is located above your emitters. After the pump is turned off, the nutrient solution will continue to siphon through the pump and down the supply line even if only one emitter is below the reservoir. You can either use an anti-siphon valve to stop this siphoning action or move the reservoir below the level of the emitter.

 Rule of Thumb: Check the solution level of the reservoir regularly and replenish with water as needed.

Water Filters

Neither your pump nor your hydroponic system will work correctly if you do not filter your nutrient solution. Filters are necessary to remove debris from an irrigation system so water can flow freely through pumps and drip emitters.

Some gardeners reap great success using homemade, inexpensive filters. You can set a simple pump basket, or a plastic kitchen scouring pad around the pump to filter out large debris. A folded nylon stocking works well to filter

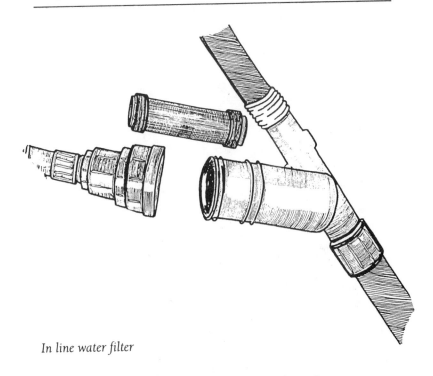

In line water filter

drain or pump intakes. Be sure to secure the nylon or scouring pad in place.

In addition to homemade alternatives, there are many filtering systems available commercially. You can have an inexpensive household water filter installed in your water line. Many people install these systems below their kitchen sink so water which comes from the tap is already filtered. When purchasing a filter, there are several options to consider. They are rated to be used with either just cold, or cold and hot water. Filters are also rated according to the size (in microns) particle they can filter. Many household systems use cotton filters which remove rust and dirt particles as small as 25 microns. A cellulose fiber filter will remove particles as small as 5 microns (two ten thousandths of an inch); and a charcoal filter will even remove bad taste and smell. Because it removes virtually everything from the water, a compressed block, activated charcoal filter is a good option. A granulated carbon filter is not recommended.

Installing a filter in your water system will keep unwanted debris out of your garden. Install a good strainer in your hydroponic system (80 mesh or smaller line filter) to remove debris that could collect and clog or plug drip emitters. One Australian nursery recommends inexpensive sponge filters. The sponge is easy to clean and very effective.For best results, clean the strainer regularly. Dirt is one of the biggest obstacles in a drip system because it sticks in the emitters. Clogged emitters flow at different rates and cause uneven irrigation. To counter this problem, be certain to install a stainless steel or plastic screen to catch debris. In addition, you can use a high pressure pump and maintain enough pressure in the system to flush any debris or salt build-up out of the nozzle. On the other hand, you can use a low pressure pump with no restrictions at the emitter.

Timers

To fully automate your system, you will need to add a timer. A timer is an essential component of a high performance garden because it ensures that your garden is irrigated on a regular schedule. For gardens that need to be irrigated more than once a day, a timer allows you flexibility because it controls the pumps and solenoid valves for you.

Although a timer which cycles for 24 hours and uses adjustable trippers to turn electrical appliances on and off is a good option for most household needs, it is not a good option for your garden. These timers generally have a minimum "on" time between 30 minutes and an hour, which is far

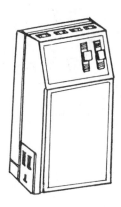

A heavy duty multi circuit timer and a simple, versatile digital timer.

too long for a rockwool garden. Cubes, slabs, and flock normally require a 15 to 30 minute irrigation cycles. Roots start
to get starved for oxygen and may die if the nutrient solution
regularly floods the rockwool for more than 15 minutes.
None-the-less, gardeners report top feed irrigating twice a day
for one half hour each irrigation with good results. Their
trick is to let lots of nutrient solution flow out the emitter
tube and use an aquarium aerator in the reservoir to add oxygen to the nutrient solution.. These practices delivers new,
oxygen-rich nutrient solution and flush away excess salts.

Because your garden should not be flooded for any-
more then 15 minutes, you will need to purchase a timer
which has a minimum "on" time of 15 minutes or less. You
can convert a 24-hour timer into an acceptable alternative by
buying either a mechanical short range or a percentage cycle
timer. Such timers are relatively expensive and need to be
used in conjunction with a 24-hour timer. The 24-hour timer

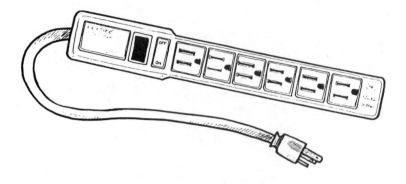

A surge protector will save pump motors and fuses from electrical fluctuations.

turns the short range timer "on", the short range timer cycles for one to fifteen minutes, then shuts off.

A digital timer can be used without the help of a 24-hour timer. Digital timers are an excellent option because they are inexpensive and provide you great flexibility. Most digital timers have a 1 minute minimum "on" time and a 23 hour maximum. They turn on and off up to four to six times a day. When you set up your system, set the timer for a minute or two longer than it takes to fill the growing bed to ensure that it completely fills.

A lawn sprinkler timer offers even more versatility than a digital timer. Naturally these timers are also more expensive. They turn on and off for a minimum of four to twelve minutes and can cycle from 4 to 30 times every 24 hours. Many gardeners think that the added control and convenience are well worth the extra expense.

Rockwool gardens are easily and efficiently irrigated with nutrient solution when controlled by a timer. Alternatively, you can let the rockwool water itself as needed.

If you set up a scale and a micro switch, the rockwool will be able to determine when it needs to be watered. Keep a sample slab of rockwool on the scale. When the (moisture) weight falls below a "trigger point", the micro switch will turn on the pump and begin the irrigation cycle.

Unless they are used for motors over 1 horsepower, pump timers usually run on 120 volt electrical circuits. Use a surge protector to guard pump motors and fuses against electrical fluctuations.

Heaters

Plants grow best if you keep your nutrient solution between 65 and 70 degrees F. You can use either an aquarium heater or soil heating cables to maintain an optimum temperature in the root zone. If the aquarium heater or heating cables are not grounded, be sure to run a ground wire. To complete the ground, attach the other end of the ground wire to a cold water pipe or metal stake that is driven into the earth. If the air temperature is higher than the water temperature, you can use an aquarium air pump/stone to raise the temperature. Always use a submersible heater large enough to heat the entire volume of water in the reservoir without burning out (see chart below). It may take several hours to raise the temperature in a large volume of solution.

10 - 30 gal, (40 - 115 liters) = 100 watt heater
30 - 60 gal. (115 - 230 liters) = 150 watt heater
60 - 120 gal. (115 - 460 liters) = 250 watt heater

Suggested watts per gallon of nutrient solution a heater should be able to heat under ideal conditions.

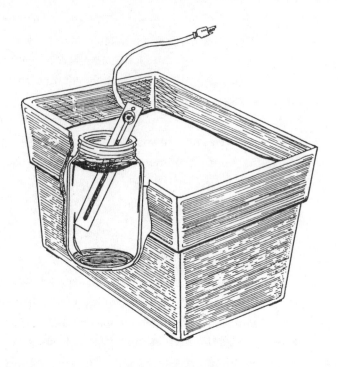

A submersible heater placed in a jar of water inside the reservoir will protect the heater from overheating should the reservoir run dry.

Submersible heaters and cables each have advantages and disadvantages. Submersible aquarium heaters have an adjustable thermostat. They are safe for fish and give off no residues that are harmful to plants. When you use a heater in your reservoir, it is all the more important to make sure that your reservoir does not run dry. If the the reservoir goes dry for more than a few minutes, your heaters may burn. The heating element, not surrounded by water, tries to heat the entire volume of air in the room. If your hydroponic system completely pumps the nutrient solution out of the reservoir, place your heater in a gallon jar full of water. This way is will not overheat if your reservoir runs dry or when cool nutrient

This grow bag is set up on a block so the cold concrete floor does not drain all the warmth out. This container will stay several degrees warmer.

solution is pumped back into the tank from the garden bed. Do not place a non-submersible heater in water. It may burn out if submerged.

Many gardeners use soil-heating cables in their rockwool gardens with great success. Many insulated soil-heating cables are equipped with a built in thermostat generally preset to about 72 degrees F (22 degrees. C). Some gardeners use these cables to heat their nutrient solution. They place the heating cables in the reservoir. The cables, even though coiled, do not overheat because the nutrient solution disperses the heat evenly. Do not, however, place the heating cables directly against the rockwool because the heat will burn roots and dry out portions of the rockwool. Always use something (a pad, or sand) to transfer the heat between the cable and the rockwool. The main restriction of using a soil-heating cable is that few are grounded. Also, heating cables heat up quickly. When the element is out of the water, do not touch it. For a large garden, use a household water heater element attached to a thermostat.

For a less mechanical system, you can rely on solar energy to heat your nutrient solution. Because water retains heat or cold for a long time, you can use water barrels painted black to absorb heat from the sun. These barrels serve as solar heat banks and can be employed in a greenhouse. Line up barrels underneath your growing benches and in a sunny location. The barrels will absorb heat during the day, and release it at night. Because water cools more slowly than air, it gives off heat. When controlling the heat in your garden, be aware that the reverse is also true. Once cold, water stays cold. Make sure that your reservoir is not getting cooled by its surroundings, a cold cement floor for example. To insulate the bottom of your reservoir, set it up on a piece of Styrofoam or wood blocks.

Finally, you can preserve heat when you change the nutrient solution by replacing the spent solution with water that is at least 60 degrees F (15 degrees C). Cold water will shock delicate roots and may take a day or two to warm up.

Irrigation Cycle

Once you have all the necessary equipment to establish a hydroponic garden, you can establish an irrigation system and schedule. There are many different ways to irrigate your garden. Some gardeners prefer the ebb and flow method, while others prefer to use a drip emitter system. Some garden beds are flooded from the top, others from the bottom. Regardless of the system you choose, to ensure a successful rockwool garden, it is important to have an efficient irrigation system.

How frequently you irrigate depends on the type and size of the plants you are growing, and on the conditions of the plants' growing environment (light, temperature, humidity). Some high performance gardens are irrigated as often as once an hour, while others are irrigated for only a few minutes one to four times a day. For instance, because roots in some ebb and flow gardens are exposed to air, they should be irrigated every hour. As a general rule, to achieve fast growth you should water your plants frequently, but in small amounts. Plants grow best with a consistent water supply. If your growing beds need more water, increase irrigation frequency as opposed to how much you water. Keep the volume of each irrigation cycle constant, but change the number of waterings to accommodate your plants' needs. For instance, you might need to water more frequently during the heat of the summer. On a hot summer day, during prime growing conditions, each mature plant may take up several quarts of water a day. You might need to irrigate your garden between 10 and 20 times a day to provide enough water and nutrients. Europeans irrigate this often year-round. They apply enough excess solution to obtain a 10 to 20 percent leaching effect daily. None-the-less, other gardeners irrigate two to four times per day; the nutrient solution flows through top feed tubing for one half hour per irrigation with good results. These gardeners suggest using an aquarium air pump to add oxygen to the nutrient solution.

Not only must you consider seasons and heat when planning your irrigations cycles, but you must also consider time of day. Although plants need water both day and night, they consume more when light and heat are more intense. Because plants do not use as much water during the night, you do not need to irrigate as frequently.

During and soon after irrigation, the nutrient content of the bed and the reservoir are virtually equal. As time passes between irrigations, the nutrient concentration and the pH level gradually change in both the slabs and the reservoir. If enough time passes between waterings, the nutrient concentration may change so drastically that plants are no longer able to absorb nutrients properly.

 Rule of Thumb: To check a cube for maximum moisture content, pick it up so that one corner is lower than the others. A few drops of nutrient solution will trickle from a block that is totally saturated.

Flood and Drain Irrigation

Flood and drain (also known as ebb and flow) gardens work by flooding the garden bed with nutrient solution. As the nutrient solution floods into the garden bed, it carries oxygen-rich air and nutrient-rich solution to the plants. At the same time, it pushes oxygen-depleted air and nutrient-depleted solution out of the garden bed and back into the reservoir where it gains potency before being recirculated back to the garden bed.

Ebb and flow technology is used extensively by commercial Dutch growers. These systems simplify the laborious chore of watering hundreds of containers with an exact supply of nutrients. A large table is used as a garden bed and alternately flooded with nutrient solution and then drained.

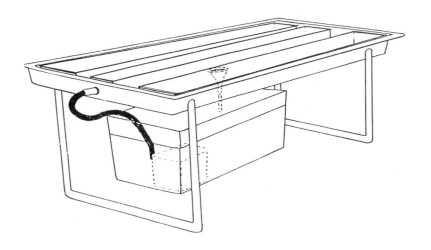

A pump pumps nutrient solution up to the table, and drains back to the reservoir.

Drain slots in the table channel the nutrient solution back to the reservoir. The Dutch realized that by using flood and drain tables, it is easy to control growth while investing very little work.

American gardeners have unknowingly used Dutch ebb and flow technology for many years. Ebb and flow technology is perfect for the frequent and consistent irrigation required by fast growing rockwool cubes or rockwool filled pots. All of the cubes absorb the nutrient solution at the same time. When using pots, the drain holes should be located on the sides rather than on the bottom to allow for better drainage.

Today, both commercial hydroponic growers and home hobbyists rely on the ebb and flow systems for high performance gardens. Because ebb and flow gardens ensure that oxygen-rich air is continuously available to plants, they produce excellent yields. As the nutrient solution floods into the garden bed, it pushes CO_2-rich, oxygen-poor air out. When the rockwool drains, it draws in new oxygen-rich air. In this way, an optimum environment is created for nutrient uptake and plant growth. Remember, the more oxygen to which a plant has access, the easier it will be for it to absorb nutrients.

Drip Irrigation

Drip irrigation revolutionized desert farming. It spread from Israel in the 60s, to California and Arizona in the 70s, and into the greenhouse industry by the 80s. Now drip irrigation is becoming a popular way to irrigate house plants and hobby gardens all across America.

In a drip irrigation system, nutrient solution is delivered to the garden bed through the work of either gravity or a pump. The nutrient solution travels from the reservoir to the garden bed via a large supply hose which is connected to either smaller spaghetti tubing or to a drip emitter.

When choosing the "workhorse" of this system, you have several factors to consider. You can choose to have a large, high volume pump, an inexpensive, low volume pump, or gravity do the work. High pressure drip emitters must be operated at a greater pressure than a small pump can generate. Low pressure drip emitters employ spaghetti tubing with little restriction at the emitter.

For large gardens of 100 emitters or more which operate on a high volume pump, labyrinth nozzles are an excellent option. Labyrinth emitters deliver the same amount of solution to each plant and do not clog easily. In addition, the pressure in the system flushes debris through the nozzles.

Many gardeners like drip systems because they can irrigate in small amounts on a regular basis. Remember, plants grow better when they are provided with frequent waterings of small quantities. Some drip systems are able to deliver a pint or less per feeding. The key to irrigating 10 to 20 times every 24 hours is having a drip system that delivers solution to all your slabs at an even rate even though the volume delivered is small.

Drip systems for rockwool slabs should deliver from .25 gallons to 1.5 gallons of solution per hour. Nutrient solution delivery can vary from 6 to 12 fluid ounces per emitter while maintaining relatively even distribution of nutrients. The incline of slabs should be at least 2 percent to ensure good nutrient flow and check each emitter to ensure that it is flowing evenly.

Many gardeners set up a small drip system and use no emitters to restrict the flow of nutrient solution. They simply run small spaghetti supply tubing to the plant and let the nutrient solution flow out the opening. The nutrient solution drains through the rockwool freely, carrying with it any excess salt build-up.

The irrigation cycle is also less frequent, two to four times per day, and longer, 30 minutes. The extra flow of nutrient solution carries extra oxygen to guard against drowning roots.

This is an excellent way to set up a very simple system that requires less maintenance and good results.

Do-It-Yourself Rockwool Gardens

Although you can purchase many kinds of hydroponic systems in garden supply stores, it is possible to create an excellent system on your own. As previously discussed, there are several basic kinds of rockwool systems, some more complicated to make and maintain than others. In this section you will find instructions on how to build several different successful hydroponic systems. We provide information on building both ebb and flow and drip emitter systems. Our goal is to help you create a basic system which will not require a major financial or time investment. You do not need to be wealthy, or a construction engineer to put together the systems we outline. Our objective is to provide first-time growers with inexpensive, easy to build, and easy to maintain alternatives.

Creating An Ebb and Flow Cube Garden

For do-it-yourself hobbyists, ebb and flow hydroponic systems are easy to create. A simple flood and drain system requires two 5-gallon plastic buckets, some gravel, and a cork. Cut a drain hole in the 5-gallon bucket which will serve as the garden bed. Fill the bucket with washed gravel and plug the drain hole with a cork. The garden bed is ready to be filled with rockwool flock and planted. Store your nutrient solution in the other 5-gallon bucket, which serves as your reservoir. To irrigate, pour the nutrient solution from the reservoir bucket into the garden bed bucket. Let it seep in for twenty to thirty minutes. When you are ready to drain the garden bed, simply place the reservoir underneath the garden bed, and pull the cork. The nutrient solution will drain back into the reservoir.

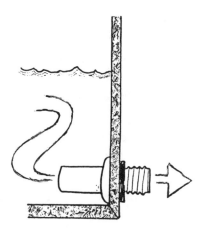

This type of fitting will keep your system from leaking. Ask your local supplier for details on the fittings they carry.

Although this system is messy and laborious, it is inexpensive and easy to create. You can elaborate on the basic principles of this system to create many different flood and drain systems. For instance, you can substitute a hose for the cork, and let gravity help you flood and drain your garden. Drill holes in each of the two 5-gallon buckets. Connect a flexible hose between the bottom of the reservoir bucket and the bottom of the growing bed. Use neoprene gasket type compression fittings to make the connections. Place the reservoir bucket below the garden bed and fill it with nutrient solution. When you want to irrigate, simply lift the reservoir bucket above the garden bed and the solution will flood into the garden bed. Let the solution stand for fifteen minutes before you lower the reservoir below the garden bed.

An automated system works on the same principle, but employs a pump and a timer instead of your labor and organization. Follow the same principles discussed above.

You reservoir must be below your garden bed and connected in some way with pipes or hoses. It is also a good idea to create an overflow line which directs excess nutrient solution back to the reservoir. Install a pump which will move the nutrient solution from the reservoir to the growing chambers via the tubing you install. To fully automate the system, attach a timer to the pump.

For large ebb and flow gardens, it is necessary to calculate how much nutrient solution the garden bed will hold and use a reservoir that will hold 25 to 50 percent more. This extra volume is the necessary to compensate for evaporation and transpiration, and to provide some leaching action.

Rockwool Wick Gardens

A rockwool wick garden works by drawing nutrient solution up from a reservoir into a garden bed. Capillary or wick action draws the nutrient solution to the roots. Wick gardens grow strong, healthy house plants such as African violets. However, for rapid growing flowers and vegetables, wick gardens generally keep the medium too wet and provide an inadequate amount of air to the roots. Wick gardens work well if they are engineered properly. They have no moving parts, a low initial cost, and few maintenance demands once set-up.

To create a rockwool wick garden, you will need two plastic containers that can stack without collapsing or locking together. Restaurant quality, high density polyethylene (HDPE) bins work well because they are strong and have a lip which prevents them from locking together. Do not choose containers that nestle too tightly together. You need enough room in the reservoir for both the nutrient solution and at

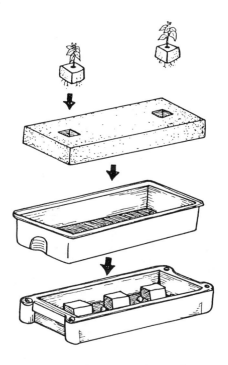

A wick garden   Note the rockwool cubes in the reservoir that are wicking the nutrient up to the slab in the bed.

least an inch of air. If your containers nestle to closely together, you will need to alter the growing chamber so that it is shallow enough, and far enough above the reservoir container.

Once you have your containers selected and modified if necessary, drill several holes in the base of the garden bed. You will need a drain hole, a hole for a filler tube, and four wick line holes. The holes for the wicking material should be scattered so the nutrient solution is wicked into a variety of places in the garden bed. The fill hole should be sized to match a PVC fitting which gets attached to a 3/4-inch PVC tubing. The drain hole simply provides an additional outlet from which the nutrient solution can flow.

Attach the PVC fitting to the base of the garden bed and thread the tube into it. The tube acts as a housing for an indicator rod, which you can make out of household objects. For instance, attach a piece of Styrofoam to a straightened wire coat hanger, and place the rod in the fill tube. The indicator rod needs to be long enough so that it reaches from the bottom of the reservoir to the top of the filler tube when the unit is assemble. The level of the indicator rod will let you know the level of the nutrient solution in the reservoir.

Polyester rope works well in wick gardens. It is available at sewing and craft stores. Cut the wicks so they are long enough to reach the bottom of reservoir without coiling up. Wet the wicking rope before you insert it into the holes in the bottom of the garden bed. Once the wicking rope is in place, you are ready to place the rockwool in your garden. Use rockwool flock at the bottom of the growing chamber to cover the holes and the wick. The more contact you can establish between the wick and the growing material, the more even the water application.

Once you have planted in your growing bed, you are ready to operate the system. Fill the reservoir about half way with nutrient solution. Place the growing chamber on top of the reservoir and water your garden. Once the garden bed has drained, check the indicator rod to determine if the reservoir is full. If it is not, use the filler line to add more nutrient solution.

This system will work automatically by wicking the nutrient solution up to the garden bed, and then draining down again through the drain hole. Check the indicator rod often to make sure you have enough solution in the reservoir. If you think your plants are getting too much water, simply tie two of the wick ends together above the water line to render them inoperable. If your plants look dry, you may need to occasionally water them from the top.

Such a system requires very little maintenance or investment. You will need to clean the garden bed and reservoir regularly. Also, check to make sure that plant roots do not grow so much that they clog the drain hole. If they do, you will need to cut them back.

For a simpler version of this system, you can use a rockwool slab on its side as a wick. Follow the same principles, but place a rockwool slab between the reservoir and the growing chamber.

A Drip System

Drip emitter systems provide an easy and efficient means by which to irrigate your slab garden. Because drip emitters supply the nutrient directly to the plants' roots, plants are able to efficiently use the nutrients they are supplied.

If you want to use a drip emitter system, it is easy to make your own. You will need two kinds of tubing, half-inch supply tubing and spaghetti tubing. Lay half-inch supply tubing along the sides of your rockwool slabs, and cut the tubing to length. If you bought stiff tubing and it is difficult to work with, set it in hot water to make it more pliable. Lay the supply tubing flat and secure it in place with plastic ties or conduit tie downs. Use a hole punch, nail, or electric drill to make holes in the half-inch supply tubing. Cut the spaghetti tubing at a 45 degree angle and insert it into the hole in the supply tubing. The spaghetti tubes should be long enough (12 to 24 inches) to reach each plant easily while remaining out of the way. Attach the other end of the tubing to the drip emitter. Secure the emitter so that it drips on the rockwool cube or slab. Be aware of the water flow. You do not want it to run out on the plastic sleeving and spill on the floor.

One dripper should be sufficient for each plant. If one dripper does not supply enough nutrient solution to a plant, add another dripper or use a dripper that supplies more volume. In fact, many gardeners do not use an emitter at all. They use small spaghetti tubing that supplies a small, but constant stream of nutrient solution.

In recirculating systems, make certain to change the nutrient solution every week or two. Changing the nutrient solution on the same day each week, makes it easier to remember.

To drain the reservoir install a "Y" in the supply hose. One end is connected to the pump and drip system and the other to a male threaded end cap that fits a garden hose.

To ensure an efficient system, you will need to flush the supply lines between crops or every 2-3 months. Use an algaecide/bactericide such as Phaisan, hydrogen peroxide, bleach, or potassium hydroxide (pH up). Run the flush through the reservoir and the supply lines. Install a valve on the end of each pipe so the solution flows through the lines and back into the reservoir. Be careful to rinse the system with a lot of fresh water to flush away the cleanser before putting the garden back into use.

Chapter Three
How a Plant
Grows in Rockwool

The Growing Medium

Now that you have a basic understanding of how a hydroponic system works and what it accomplishes, you must consider how rockwool plays a role in that system to promote plant growth. All growing media, soil and soilless alike, must preform certain functions in order to foster plant growth. A growing medium must provide a place for roots to grow so they can anchor a plant. The growing material must not only support the roots, but it must also possess an optimum structure which promotes the proper absorption and drainage of water so roots can breathe. If a growing medium drains too quickly, roots will not be able to absorb enough water and nutrients to feed the plant. On the other hand, if the growing medium drains too slowly, the roots will not be able to absorb enough oxygen. Without oxygen, a plant can not assimilate the nutrients it is provided. Finally, a growing medium must supply, or act as a reservoir for, the nutrients which a plant needs to thrive.

Because of its unique characteristics, rockwool successfully meets these criteria of a productive growing medium. Providing the proper growing material is only the first step in the process of growing a successful indoor garden. Remember, rockwool does not naturally contain water, or any nutrients. It only acts as a container, holding these crucial elements within a plant's reach. It is up to the gardener to supply adequate water, oxygen, and nutrients. In this chapter, you will gain an understanding of how a plant lives, grows, and reproduces itself. Understanding these life processes of a plant will help you to understand your role as a gardener. For instance, knowing how a root functions in a plant's life will help you to understand why it is so important that you keep the root zone moist, but not soggy. This chapter gives you the background you will need to understand the importance of the next chapter, which outlines the role of water and nutrients in a plant's life.

The Growing Process

Plant seeds have an outside coating which protects the embryo plant and encases a supply of food. Given moisture, heat, and air, a healthy seed will germinate. As the seed begins to germinate, it splits its outer coating. A rootlet forms and grows downward in search of water and nutrients, while a sprout with seed leaves pushes upwards in search of light.

The single root from the seed grows down and branches out, similar to the way the stem branches out above ground. Tiny rootlets draw in water and nutrients. Roots

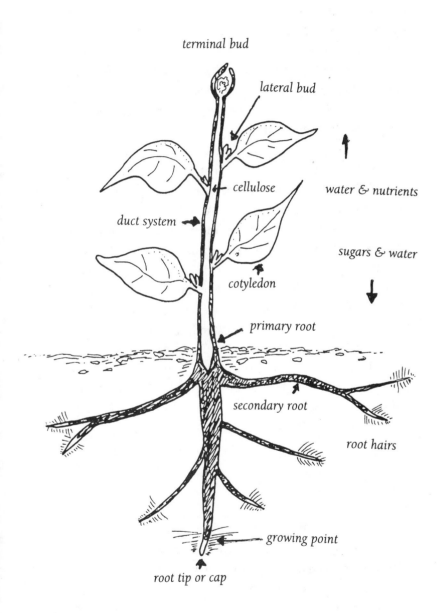

Cut away drawing of a plant that explains how it grows.

also anchor plants in their growing medium. As the plant matures, the roots take on specialized functions. The center and more mature portions of the root contain a water transport system. These older root sections may also store food. The tips of the roots produce elongating cells that continue to push farther and farther into the rockwool in a quest for more water and food. It is the single-celled root hairs that actually absorb the water and nutrients. These root hairs depend on the presence of water and oxygen to preserve their life. Without these two essential elements, the root hairs will dry up and die. They are very delicate and may easily be damaged by light, air, or careless hands.

By producing new buds, the stem also grows through an increase in the total number of cells. The central or terminal bud carries growth upward, while side or lateral buds form branches and leaves. The stem transmits water and nutrients from the delicate root hairs to the growing buds, leaves, and flowers. Sugars and starches, manufactured in the leaves, are distributed through the plant via the stem. This fluid flow takes place near the surface of the stem. If the stem is bound too tightly by string or other tie-downs, it will cut the flow of life-giving fluids. The stem also supports the plant with stiff cellulose, located in the inner walls.

Photosynthesis

Once the leaves expand, they start to manufacture food (carbohydrates). Chlorophyll, the substance that gives plants their green color, converts air, water, nutrients, and light energy into carbohydrates and oxygen. This process, known as photosynthesis, only takes place in the presence of

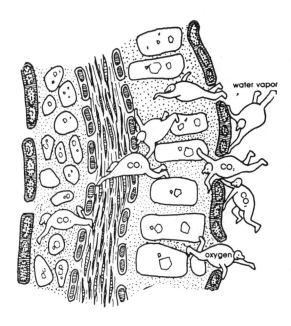

Stomata on leaf underside.

carbon dioxide (CO_2). During the photosynthetic process, water is drawn up from the roots, through the stem, and into the leaves where it encounters CO_2. Tiny pores located on the top and underside of the leaf, called stomata or stoma, funnel CO_2 into contact with the water. In order for photosynthesis to occur, the leaf's interior tissue must be kept moist. The stomata prevent dehydration by opening and closing to regulate the flow of moisture. Plant leaves also possess an outer skin which helps protect them from drying out. In addition to regulating moisture flow, stomata permit the outflow of water vapor and oxygen. Because the stomata perform such important functions, they must be kept clean at all times to promote vigorous growth.

Photoperiodism (Phytochrome Responses)

Photosynthesis is only one of several crucial plant growth factors. Light also affects plant growth through a process known as photoperiodism. The length of daylight, known as the photoperiod, determines flowering, seed formation, stem lengthening, leaf growth and color, and bulb and tuber formation. It is actually the absence of light that determines these plant growth factors. Contrary to previous belief, scientists have now proven that the duration of darkness, not light, stimulates plant functions.

Historically plants have been classified according to the amount of daylight they require. Long-day plants such as grains, many vegetables, most annual flowers, require 14-18 hours of light to accumulate optimum amounts of florigen. Short-day plants such as Napa cabbage, poinsettias, chrysanthemum, and gardenias rely on 10-13 hours of light to produce florigen. Long-day/short-day plants such as *Callistephus Sinensis,* require a specific light cycle of long days followed by short days to bloom. Day-neutral plants are theoretically not effected by the duration of light. However, day-neutral plants may flower more with more light because of increases in photosynthesis. In addition, day-neutral plants are sensitive to day and night temperature variations. This is called thermoperiodism. Turning off lamps at night decreases the air temperature which triggers flowering. Although many gardeners still classify their plants according to daylight requirements, it is more accurate to classify them according to darkness requirements. Short-day plants are actually long-night plants and long-day plants are actually short-night plants. If even a minimal amount of light interrupts the dark period of long-night plants, their flowering can be stunted. Many gardeners use short bursts of light to interrupt darkness to delay flowering and control growth. When possible, it is best to group plants together according to their daylight requirements.

The majority of plants are long-day and bloom according to chronological age. That is, when they are two or three months old, they start to bloom. Flowers such as marigolds, petunias, pansies, cosmos, California poppies, and zinnias will continue to bloom once flowering starts. Long-day vegetables set blossoms that drop when fruit form. Many common vegetables such as tomatoes, peppers, eggplant, and squash fall into this category.

Plant Gender

Plant "gender" affects the way in which plants reproduce themselves. Monoecious plants have (a) both male and female reproductive organs on the *same* individual or (b) are plants having unisexual, male and female flowers on the *same* plant. Many times the term "hermaphrodite" is used to describe this type of plant. However, "hermaphrodite" is a term reserved for the animal world. Gardeners can spur pollination by shaking a plant. Seeds on a dioecious plant form and grow within the female flowers.

Dioecious plants have both male and female organs located on *different* individual plants.

Gynoecious plants have only female flowers such as seedless cucumbers.

The Roots

From this brief description of plant growth and reproduction, it is easy to see that each part of a plant—roots, stem,

leaves, flower, and fruit—performs a function crucial to plant
vigor. No part could support plant health without the help of
the others. However, the first step to plant growth is providing a healthy root environment. Without healthy roots, a
plant would not be able to support itself in its growing medium or absorb water or nutrients. Without water, air, light or
nutrients, a plant can not perform any of the other functions
which are so vital to its life. Although providing a healthy
environment for roots is only the first of many essential steps
in growing a high performance garden, it is what we will focus
on in the next chapter.

Chapter Four
Water and Nutrients

Introduction

Water and nutrients are two mainstays of plant health. Without one or the other, a plant will die. Remember, when you garden indoors, you assume the responsibility of providing a plant with all its needs. You must take over and become Mother Nature. In order to understand how to best control water and nutrient supply, you must first understand their functions within a plant. In the following chapter you will find a discussion of how water and nutrients work together to build the basis for plant life. In addition, you will find a detailed discussion about how to control these factors when gardening indoors with rockwool.

Water

When you are establishing a hydroponic garden using rockwool as your growing medium, you must remember the

importance of water. Thus far we have focused on the importance of rockwool and the role it plays in plant growth.
Rockwool is successful largely because of its ability to support
plant roots, deliver water, nutrient solution, and air.

Because there is so much air space between the fibers
of rockwool, it is able to hold ample air, water, and nutrient
solution. In fact, even when rockwool is saturated, the ratio
of water to air within the pores of the growing medium is ideal
for root growth. When fully wet, some brands of rockwool
contain approximately eighty percent nutrient solution, fifteen percent air pore space, and five percent rockwool fiber.
This ratio allows plants to easily absorb water and nutrients
while still having adequate access to oxygen.

Water and fertilizer work together to feed plants and
promote healthy growth. Nutrients in fertilizer dissolve in
water to form a nutrient solution. This water based solution
carries nutrients through the plant. Tiny root hairs absorb
the water, nutrients, and oxygen in the solution and carry
them, via the stem, to the leaves. This passive flow of water
from the substrate through the plant is known as transpiration. A fraction of the water absorbed by the root hairs is
processed and used in photosynthesis; the remainder evaporates via the stomata into the air. As the water evaporates it
carries waste products with it. Some of the water also carries
manufactured sugars and starches to the roots.

Rockwool has a broad range of water-holding capaci-
ties. It acts like a water bank for the roots. Water is deposited
or saved until needed, then it is withdrawn from the rockwool
by the roots.

One hobby gardener reported that while away on
vacation, the electricity went off at her home. Her rockwool
garden was not irrigated for eight days and nights. Although
the plants growing in the slabs were alive upon her return,

they had not grown much. They also suffered from mild fertilizer burn. She changed the nutrient solution and watered a double cycle to flush out salt build-up and ensure complete wetting of the slabs. The garden took off to grow a fine crop.

Although rockwool is forgiving, you do need to care for it to ensure a healthy garden. Be certain not to over-water plants grown in rockwool. With proper drainage, rockwool holds more than enough air to speed nutrient uptake. However, if your system does not drain properly, or if you are not careful, it is possible to over-water rockwool. Over-watering can drown roots and cut off their oxygen supply. If roots stand in stagnant puddles of water for over a few hours they may rot.

Water Quality

Although the water from most local systems is sufficient, tap water can contain elements which are detrimental to plant growth. Household tap water may contain high levels of alkaline salts, sulfur, chlorine, or sodium which can damage your garden. In addition, your tap water may have a pH out of the optimal range of 5.5 to 6.5. While sulphur is easy to detect because of its distinct taste and smell, saline is more difficult to recognize. Most water supplies contain both sodium and chlorine.

For the most part, these elements are present in water in acceptable quantities. However, if you live on the coast or in a lakeside community, or if your water is softened, your water may contain too much chlorine and/or sodium to be safely used in your garden. Water in coastal areas is generally full of salts that wash inland from the ocean. Many present day deserts are ancient lake beds where vast deposits of salts have built-up. Water from these areas will be full of undesirable salts. These salts, usually calcium and iron, are easy to detect because they often build-up around shower heads and household water taps.

Chlorine and sodium are added to many "soft" water systems. Although small amounts of chlorine affect plant growth very little, salt-softened water should be avoided. Because plants use only minute quantities of chlorine, your rockwool will harbor deposits unless you flush regularly. Excess salt will kill your plants. When sodium and chlorine build-up in the rockwool, they increase the conductivity factor (CF) of the medium. At the higher CF, the plants take up sodium instead of vital potassium, calcium, and magnesium.

 Rule of Thumb: Nutrient solution water should contain very low Conductivy Factor (salts).

While soft water can occasionally cause problems, hard water is usually good for gardens. Hard or well water may be very alkaline and usually contains notable amounts of calcium and magnesium. Both nutrients will be put to good use by flowering and fruiting plants. Hard (alkaline) water seldom contains enough calcium or magnesium to toxify rockwool. However, if the pH climbs above 7, the calcium can combine with the magnesium sulfate to create gypsum, which is insoluble and renders the nutrients useless to the plants.

Because tap water can contain harmful ingredients, it is advisable to request a water analysis from your local water bureau. If the sodium and chlorine register less than 50 parts per million (ppm) you probably have little about which to worry. If the level is between at 50 and 70 ppm, the stage is set for nutrient problems. If the chlorine or sodium content is above 100, do not use the water without filtrating it. If neces-

	Maximum	Minimum
pH	4.0	8.0
conductivity (DS) - less than 100 ppm, .09 EC		
Nitrate-nitrogen	10	500
Phosphorus	40	100
Potassium	100	600
Calcium	100	600
Magnesium	50	150
Sodium	0	400
Chlorine	10	200
Sulfur	150	1000
Iron	0.5	5
Copper	0.5	1
Zinc	0.1	1
Manganese	0.5	10
Boron	0.1	1
Molybdenum	0.001	05
Bicarbonate equivalent - 45 - 60 ppm HCO_3		

Minimum and maximum mineral concentrations for fertilizer solution: The nutrient each nutrient in the solution should fall within this range for healthy plant growth

sary, a reverse osmosis(RO) machine could be your salvation. Unfortunately, filtering can be an expensive proposition. For a simple and inexpensive way to remove chlorine from water, let it sit overnight in an open container. The chlorine will turn to gas and evaporate. Heating or stirring the solution dissipates the chlorine faster. If you determine that your tap water is not conducive to plant growth, you can also consider using distilled water or rain water if it is clean. An increasing number of locations in the world are unable to use their rain water because it is not "pure". Acid rain is rainwater that is full of airborne acidic pollutants that dissolve in water.

The nutrients listed in a water analysis from your local water bureau should not possesses any nutrients in excessively high levels. If excessive levels of specific nutrients occur, consider using another water source or use a fertilizer that has a minimal amount of the abundant nutrient.

Once you have determined the make-up of your water, you can begin formulating an appropriate nutrient solution for your plants. If you want a fine-tuned garden and total control, start with pure (filtered) water and add all the appropriate soluble nutrients to the solution. This is easily done if you use a commercial "complete" plant nutrient specifically designed for growing in rockwool.

If you are using "unpure" tap water, you can still maintain control over the nutrient content of your rockwool garden. After you read your water analysis, you will be able to mix a nutrient solution to compliment your water and your crop. For more information on preparing nutrient solutions talk to an expert at a garden supply store.

Whether you use tap water or filtered water it is essential to flush your garden regularly. Even if you are using "clean" water, the potential exists for minerals and salts to build up. Excessive sodium, chlorine, and sulfates can inhibit seed germination, stunt plant growth, and burn root hairs, tips, and edges of leaves. Salt build-up in rockwool is easily controlled by regularly leaching your garden with a weak nutrient solution. Leach at the rate of 15 - 20 percent overdrain on a 3 - 4-hour basis and 40 - 60 percent overdrain during peak solar (light) period (10 AM - 2 PM). It is a good idea to leach containers every week, slabs daily, and house plants monthly. A 10 to 30 percent overflow or flooding every week usually prevents fertilizer salt build-up.

This salt build up on a houseplant container is your first clue that your water has excess dissolved salts in it.

Some hobby gardens are located in area which will not accommodate free run-off. Hobbyists with small gardens have found recirculating the nutrient solution works well. Be sure to top off the reservoir every few days with water or a mild mix of nutrient solution and change the solution weekly. The nutrient solution should be completely drained and changed every week or two if recirculation is used.

The Nutrient Solution

In a hydroponic garden, water is not important only for its own sake. It is equally important because it serves as the vehicle which distributes nutrients to plants. When fertilizer is dissolved in water, it creates a nutrient solution which feeds plants. Because rockwool does not possess any of its own nutrients (as soil-based media do), gardeners have complete control over the make-up of their plants' nutrient supply. Most gardeners prefer to purchase balanced solutions already prepared, and a few gardeners prefer to formulate their own. If your water source is unpure, or if your plants have specific needs, formulating your own nutrient solution can be added insurance for a healthy crop.

The idea behind a rockwool nutrient solution is simple: apply a mild nutrient solution that constantly supplies plants with nutrients in an available form. Excess nutrients are flushed away with the new nutrient solution brought in with each irrigation cycle. Nutrients, therefore, never get a chance to concentrate or build-up.

 Rule of Thumb: Measure the pH of your water, adjust the pH to 5.5 to 6.0 before adding fertilizer.

A hydroponic nutrient solution supplies all the food plants need. The rate at which the nutrient solution is taken up by the plant dictates the growth rate, provided that all the plants other needs are fulfilled. Nutrient uptake is fastest when adequate oxygen is available to the roots. After the nutrient solution is applied to the rockwool, it drains away and provides air pockets. In this way, the oxygen can work with the roots to draw in the nutrients. To aerate the nutrient solution (give it more oxygen) simply pour it through the air. Every time water moves through the air, it picks up oxygen. An aquarium air stone or bubbler can also be placed in the reservoir for added aeration.

A Basic Nutrient Solution Recipe

For a basic nutrient solution, you can follow the recipe below. You may need to alter it to accommodate any excesses in your water supply, or deficiencies in your plants. This recipe is based on 120 gallons. For small gardens, alter the quantities proportionately.

In a container mix a formula consisting of:

20 ounces potassium nitrate,
10 ounces calcium nitrate,
15 ounces superphosphate,
5 ounces magnesium sulfate.

In a separate container, combine the trace elements. You may need to use a mortar and pestle to grind them to a fine powder. Mix:

1 ounce iron sulfate,
1 teaspoon manganese sulfate,
1/2 teaspoon boric acid powder,
1/2 teaspoon zinc sulfate,
1/2 teaspoon copper sulfate.

Add this powder to the formula. Use 1/2 teaspoon per 100 gallons of water, or dissolve 1/2 teaspoon in one quart of water and use one liquid ounce to three gallons of nutrient solution. Mix only what you need, as the leftovers should be discarded.

Nutrients and Nutrient Disorders

Nutrients are the substance of plant food. Properly balancing the nutrients in your nutrient solution will feed your plants and prevent toxic build-ups. Plants rely on over twenty nutrients for healthy growth. With the exception of carbon, hydrogen, and oxygen which a plant absorbs from the air, all nutrients must be supplied to a plant in a nutrient solution.

Providing optimum nutrient levels to plants is crucial if you want to grow a successful garden. Rockwool gardens can be very high-performance, creating phenomenal plant growth. However, if something malfunctions, for instance if the electricity goes off, the pump breaks, the drain gets clogged with roots, or pH fluctuates rapidly, plant growth could slow to a halt. A repeated mistake could kill or stunt plants so badly that they never fully recover. The key to a successful high-performance rockwool gardens is providing the proper amount of nutrients to plants. Starving or over-feeding your plants can potentially cause slowed growth and ultimately death.

Nutrient disorders are caused by an excess or deficiency of one or several nutrients. Nutrients are only available to plants if you maintain the pH between 5.5 and 6.5. Maintaining these conditions is the key to proper nutrient uptake and is a necessary measure to prevent nutrient deficiencies and excesses. A pH fluctuation could create a nutrient deficiency. Likewise, a nutrient imbalance could create a pH change. Nutrients are taken-up at different rates by plants. This uneven nutrient uptake gives some nutrients in the solution a chance to build up to toxic levels. It may be difficult to determine the exact cause of a nutrient disorder.

Nutrients move within plants in two different ways. An understanding of these forms of movement is essential to diagnosing nutrient deficiencies or excesses. They are:

1. The role of a specific nutrient within a plant
2. The ability of the nutrient to be translocated from one part of the plant to the other.

What if two or more elements are deficient (or toxic) at the same time? When difficult-to-diagnose problems occur, change the nutrient solution. In all likelihood, this will correct the problem and supply the missing elements. Rockwool acts like a large sponge that absorbs nutrients. Nutrients stay in the rockwool until roots absorb them like soap stays in a sponge. Flushing these nutrients out regularly, like flushing or wringing soap from a sponge, will help prevent nutrient imbalances. Although it is possible to have a sample of your nutrient solution and plant tissue analyzed in a laboratory so an exact nutrient mix can be formulated for your garden, this is an expensive and time-consuming alternative. It is more time and cost-effective to try to diagnose the problem yourself, or simply change your nutrient solution. A Conductivy Factor (CF) meter can be useful to determine if you have a toxic salt build-up. To avoid nutrient build-ups you can also let the nutrient solution drain to waste before changing it. Catch the "waste" nutrient solution to use on your house plants or outdoor garden. Flushing your garden regularly also helps prevent toxic build-ups.

If, after changing the nutrient solution, the problem persists, try a new fertilizer mix. Because plants sometimes respond to nutrient changes slowly, it may take up to a week for the garden to respond to a fresh or new nutrient mix. Be patient.

Rule of Thumb: If the garden has a nutrient disorder, change the nutrient solution and adjust the pH.

Although nutrient disorders do not necessarily have to be diagnosed to be treated, gardeners have identified some common and easily remedied problems of which to be aware. Look for dry pockets in the rockwool root zone. Check for even wetting and drainage. Look for fungus and insect damage on the roots and leaves respectively. The roots should be white or light tan with fine root hairs. Brown, black, or "jellylike" roots are signs of root disease. If they are receiving the same solution, nutrient disorders will occur to all plants in the garden at the same time. Climactic disorders such as windburn, lack of light, temperature stress, fungus and insect damage, usually show up on the individual plants that are most affected. For example, plants that are next to a heating vent may show signs of heat scorch.

In the following pages you will find a list of nutrients essential to plant growth and the toxicity and deficiency signs associated with each. Nutrients are classified in several categories, organized on the basis of how necessary they are to plant growth.

Macro-nutrients

Nitrogen (N), phosphorus (P) and potassium (K) are referred to as primary or macro-nutrients because they are the elements plants use most.

Nitrogen is essential to the production of amino acids, proteins and chlorophyll molecules which are causes new cell growth. Nitrogen helps establish healthy leaf and stem growth, as well as overall plant size and vigor. Nitrogen moves easily (translocates) to active young buds, shoots, and leaves, but moves more slowly to older leaves.

Older leaves display nitrogen deficiency because nitrogen is being actively moved from the older leaves to young leaves. Nitrogen deficiency causes plant leaves to turn pale yellow. A more long term deficiency will cause growth to stagnate. New growth becomes weak and spindly. An abundance of nitrogen, on the other hand, will cause dark green, soft, weak growth. If a gardener allows nitrogen to accumulate, his or her crops will experience delayed flower and fruit production.

Phosphorus works as a catalyst for energy transfer within a plant, and a stimuli for photosynthesis. In addition, phosphorus helps establish strong roots and vital flower and seed production. Phosphorous is used most during germination, seedling growth, and flowering. This macro-nutrient is mobile within the plant, so deficiency symptoms normally appear in the lower leaves near the bottom or middle of the plant first.

Phosphorus deficiency is seen first in youngest tissue, usually the underside of leaf. Leaves turn deep green, and produce brown or purple spots, while overall plant growth is uniformly slowed or stunted. When you are mixing your nutrient solution, be aware that phosphorus flocculates (turns to a solid and settles to the bottom) when it is combined with calcium. Once a phosphorus deficiency is established, it can take more than a month to stop, and even longer to remedy!

An excess phosphorous causes accelerated root growth and fewer growing tips are produced.

Potassium activates the manufacture and movement of sugars and starches and triggers the production of disease-fighting enzymes. It increases chlorophyll in foliage, and helps regulate stomata openings so plants can make better use of air. In addition, potassium encourages strong root growth, water uptake, and growth by cell division. Although potassium is necessary during all stages of growth, it is especially important in the development of fruit.

Potassium deficiencies are usually caused by high salinity. Saline build-ups prohibit potassium from reaching plants. Although many potassium deficient plants remain tall and healthy, there are several symptoms to help you identify a potassium-low garden. Potassium deficiency is first seen by leaf edge chlorosis. Eventually, since potassium is mobile within the plant, entire leaves will turn dark yellow and subsequently die. In addition, potassium deficient plants often drop there fruit and flowers.

Secondary Nutrients

Magnesium (Mg) and calcium (Ca) are referred to as secondary nutrients because they are used by plants in smaller amounts than are nitrogen, phosphorus, and potassium. Although they are used less, secondary nutrients are still crucial to plant growth.

Magnesium: Plants rely on magnesium for light absorption. In fact, magnesium is a central atom in the chlorophyll molecule. In addition, magnesium helps plants utilize nutrients and neutralize acids and toxic compounds produced by the plant. Magnesium is also involved in the process of distributing phosphorus throughout plants.

Magnesium-deficient plants often loose their vibrant greenness, because magnesium is a light-absorbing nutrient also found in chlorophyll. Older leaves will mottle and turn yellow between their veins due to export of magnesium to the upper parts of the plant. If the magnesium deficiency progresses to the top of the plant, growing tips will turn lime green.

Calcium helps stimulate the manufacturing and growth of cells. In addition, calcium fosters root development. Soil gardeners often use dolomite lime to keep the soil sweet or buffered because it contains calcium and magnesium.

Unlike most other nutrient-deficiencies, a calcium deficiency is apparent in young growth first. Young leaf tips might also discolor and curl upward. Calcium cannot be translocated from old tissue to young tissue. This is why deficiencies occur almost exclusively in young leaves first. Consequently, young growth shows signs of deficiency first. Leaf tips and edges, and new growth will turn brown and die in calcium-deficient plants The meristem growth is the most affected. Too much calcium can be as harmful as too little. Plants that receive too much calcium while they are young will be stunted. When adding calcium to your nutrient solution, remember that when combined with potassium, concentrated calcium will fluctuate.

Trace Elements

Iron (Fe), sulfur (S), manganese (Mn), boron (B), molybdenum (Mo), zinc (Zn) and copper (Cu), known as micro-nutrients or trace elements, are also necessary for healthy plant growth. Soil gardeners usually do not have to worry about trace elements because they naturally occur in most soils. Because neither rockwool nor water contain sufficient quantities of trace elements, rockwool gardeners must purchase a fertilizer which contains them, or add them to a homemade nutrient solution.

Sulphur is necessary to plants because it is a component of plant protein. It therefore plays an important role in root growth and chlorophyll supply. In addition, sulphur increases the effectiveness of phosphorus. Although sulfur is distributed relatively evenly within plants, the greatest concentration occurs in the leaves. This large concentration in the leaves affects the flavor and odor of many plants.

Sulphur, like calcium, moves little within plant tissue. Plants, therefore, show their first deficiency signs in their leaves. Young leaves turn pale, grow brittle, and remain narrower than is typical. In addition, overall plant growth slows.

Iron serves as a key catalyst for chlorophyll production, and is used in photosynthesis. If iron is lacking, leaves turn pale yellow or white while veins remain green. Because iron is difficult for plants to absorb, and because it moves slowly within a plant, always use chelated (immediately available to the plant) iron in your nutrient mix.

Manganese works with plant enzymes to reduce nitrates before plants produce proteins. Manganese also helps with the process of distributing phosphorus throughout plants. A lack of manganese turns young leaves mottled yellow or brown.

Because zinc is a catalyst, it must be present in minute amounts for plant growth. It is a vital helper in a plant's process of transferring energy. A lack of zinc results in stunted, yellow, and curled small leaves. It is uncommon to have a problem with excess zinc. If you do, it can be extremely toxic to your garden. Plants will wilt and ultimately die.

Copper is a catalyst for several enzymes and a necessary element in the production of chlorophyll. A shortage of copper causes new growth to wilt and grow irregularly. A copper excess will cause sudden death in your plants. Because of this toxic property, copper is used as a fungicide to ward off insects and diseases.

Boron is necessary both for cell division and protein formation. In addition, it plays an active role in pollination and seed production.

Molybdenum helps form proteins and aids a plant's ability to fix nitrogen from the air. A deficiency causes leaves to turn pale, and to appear scorched at the fringes. Irregular leaf growth may also result.

Although aluminum, chlorine, cobalt, iodine, selenium, silicon, sodium, and vanadium are not normally included in nutrient mixes, they also play a role in plant development. Unless your water analysis indicates otherwise, you will not have to mix these nutrients into your nutrient solution because they are usually present as impurities in the water supply. In addition, they are often mixed into other commercially available nutrients.

If you do not have any special plant needs or water impurities to balance, you can purchase commercially available nutrient mixes which contain all of these essential nutrients. These mixes contain all the necessary nutrients balanced in a ratio which will give plants what they need to stimulate lush, rapid growth. Fertilizers should be dissolved in water to form a liquid nutrient solution.

Fertilizers

Fertilizers form the base of nutrient solutions because they provide the nutrients which are necessary for plant growth. The objective of fertilization is to provide a constant supply of all necessary nutrients in optimum ratios. When the fertilizer is dissolved in water to form a nutrient solution, the nutrients become available to plants. To determine what fertilizer best suits your garden needs, you need to know how to determine the nutrient content of a given fertilizer.

Most fertilizers list nutrients by their abbreviations. For instance, the primary nutrients, nitrogen, phosphorus, and potassium, are listed as N-P-K. The primary nutrients are always listed in the same order and express the percentage of each nutrient contained in the fertilizer. For example, a fertilizer that shows 23-19-17 has 23 percent (N) nitrogen, 19 percent (P) phosphorus and 17 percent (K) potassium. The secondary and trace elements are usually listed in the "Guaranteed Analysis" on the label of the fertilizer. When choosing a fertilizer, look for one that offers a balanced and complete formula, and one that contains all the macro and micro-nutrients.

There are many good hydroponic fertilizers from which to choose. Peter's Hydrosol, EcoGrow, Rockwool Formula One, Genesis, Hydrolife, DynaGro, and General Hydroponics are examples of a few brand-name hydroponic fertilizers. There are many different hydroponic fertilizers. We recommend that you experement with several and choose the one that works the best for you. Many rockwool fertilizers are two part formulas. One part contains the phosphate source, while the other part contains the calcium source. Calcium and phosphorus must be kept separate when concentrated. Although they do not cause any problems when in diluted solutions, in a concentrated form, the two will flocculate, or combine into a worthless mud that settles on the bottom of the reservoir.

 Rule of Thumb: Use a two or three part nutrient solution for high performance gardens.

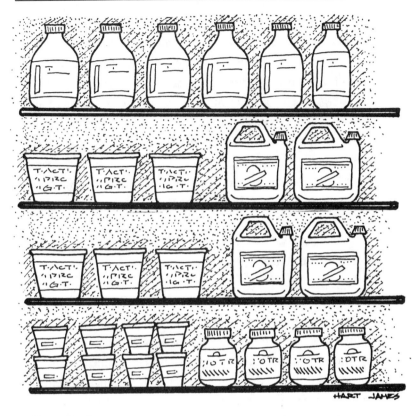

Different fertilizers.

Any complete fertilizer will work in a rockwool garden. Several specialty rockwool fertilizers are made by smaller manufacturers and some growers mix their own. If you use over 250 pounds of fertilizer per year, it is more cost-effective to mix your own. However, if you do not need such a large quantity, commercially available pre-mixed fertilizers are formulated by professionals and are easier to use. Because slow growing house plants are not as fussy as fast growing annual flowers and vegetables, some gardeners mix their own simple fertilizer for their house plants. A simple all purpose house plant fertilizer mix can be made by combining soluble trace elements with a soluble general purpose fertilizer to form a complete fertilizer. Be sure the "Guaranteed Analysis" on the fertilizer label contains at least 10 or 11 natural elements. When buying or preparing fertilizer mixes, remember that "chelated" nutrients are immediately available to the plant and speed nutrient uptake.

Whatever fertilizer you decide to use, keep it dry! The fertilizer will combine and separate into worthless slop if you allow it to get wet. Store it in a cool dry place and always read the directions completely before using.

Organic Fertilizers

Although organic fertilizers can be used to fertilize rockwool gardens, they are not used as commonly as their chemical counterparts. Chemically, the difference between organic and chemical fertilizers is minimal. While organic nutrients contain a carbon molecule, non-organic nutrients do not. Once the organic fertilizer is taken up by the roots, the organic nutrients are changed to mineral elements and compounds. Although the chemical difference between organic and chemical fertilizers is small, some gardeners prefer organic fertilizers because of environmental and health comparisons. Chemical fertilizers mixed in run-off water add to polluted ground water, damaged vegetation, and diseased animals. Similarly, some gardeners prefer not to eat plants with chemical remnants.

Although there are several arguable advantages to using organic fertilizers, there are also several detriments. Some organic nutrients are difficult to dissolve. In addition, it is more difficult for gardeners to control and analyze available minerals in organic fertilizers.

Bat guano is one of the best high phosphorus water soluble organic fertilizers available on the market.

Many organic fertilizers on the market today are made from bat and seabird guano, livestock manures, fish emulsion, and liquid seaweed because these substances are water soluble. However, seabird guano, fish emulsion, and poultry manures have the potential to be dangerously high in nitrogen and should be used sparingly. If you use an organic fertilizer, you must mix it with water and strain it through a cheese cloth or a nylon stocking before applying it to rockwool. The straining ensures that the organic tea, or nutrient solution, will not contain large chunks of insoluble elements which can plug narrow tubing or emitters. Plants extract and process mineral elements from organic materials. Unused elements must be flushed out.

Temperature

For your garden to perform at its peak, you must keep your nutrient solution between 65 and 70 degrees F (21 degrees C). Heating the nutrient solution during cool months will help boost plant performance. For every 10 degree F (5 degrees C) increase in nutrient solution heat, the rate of photosynthesis doubles. Do not let the nutrient solution temperature rise higher than 85 degrees F (30 degrees C). If roots get too hot or cold, they do not perform properly and may get damaged.

 Rule of Thumb: Every 10 degree F (5 degree C) increase in nutrient solution heat, the rate of photosynthesis doubles. Do not let the nutrient solution temperature rise higher than 85 degrees F (30 degrees C).

Chapter Five
pH and
Conductivity Factor

Growing a successful rockwool garden depends on many factors. You first need to buy or build a hydroponic system which will adequately house your plants. You need to set up an irrigation schedule to provide your plants with water, nutrients, and oxygen. Given your water quality and plants' needs, you must also purchase or mix a nutrient solution to nourish your plants.

In this chapter we discuss the role that pH and Conductivity Factor play in plant health. Even if you have taken great care in establishing an optimum system and solution, if the pH or CF are out of balance, your hard work will be futile. It is vital for plant health that you understand how pH and CF levels effect your plants, and how you can control them. In this chapter you will find a detailed discussion of how to read pH and CF levels, and how to identify and remedy imbalances. In addition, this chapter outlines the equipment you will need to successfully control the pH and CF level of your rockwool garden.

pH

pH is a scale, ranging from 1 to 14, that measures acid-to-alkaline balance. Whereas 1 is the most acidic, 7 is neutral, and 14 is the most alkaline. The pH level of your garden is an important factor to monitor because it can greatly enhance or hinder plant growth, depending on where in the range your garden falls. Most plants grown in rockwool will thrive if the pH is between 5.5 and 6.5. Within this range, most plants can absorb and process available nutrients.

If the pH is too low, or acidic, nutrients become chemically bound by acid salts. Plant roots are not able to absorb nutrients in this bound form. An alkaline growing medium, with a high pH, will cause chemical lock-up, nutrient lockout, and possible toxic salt build-up. This condition limits roots' water intake.

In addition, roots take up different nutrients at different rates. Fluctuations in the concentration of nutrients in the solution will change the pH. If the pH is not within the acceptable hydroponic range, nutrients will not be absorbed properly and growth will be slowed.

Measuring Tools

There are several ways to measure pH. Most nurseries sell litmus paper, liquid pH test kits, and electronic pH testers, all of which measure pH. Each, of course, has benefits and detriments. Regardless of which method you choose, when you test pH, and where you test it, you need to take two or three samples to get an accurate reading. Before starting your test, make sure to read and understand the directions. Use a buffer solution of known pH once a month to calibrate your measuring equipment, if necessary.

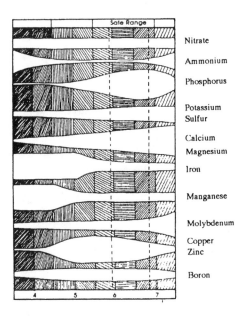

This pH chart shows the range in which nutrients are available.

The major benefit of litmus paper is its low price, while the major drawback of this method is its potential for inaccuracy. If the fertilizer you are testing contains a color agent, the litmus paper could register a false reading. In addition, litmus paper, when compared to an electronic digital pH pen, is difficult to use. Different types of litmus papers test different ranges of pH. Use litmus paper that tests a pH range of at least 4.5 to 6.5. Wet the litmus paper for 10 seconds with the solution you want to measure. The litmus paper will register a color which indicates the pH level of the solution. To understand the reading, the color of the litmus paper must be matched with an explanatory color chart.

A pH meter actually measures electrical volts. While pure water produces no currents, acidic and alkaline water produce electricity. A pH meter measures this electrical current to provide a pH reading. Inexpensive electronic pH meters are relatively accurate and very convenient. These easy-to-use electronic pH testers are available in garden centers and hardware stores. For a slightly greater investment, you can get a pH tester, or "pH pen", that is easily calibrated to ensure accuracy. Many gardeners find the extra cost to be a worthwhile investment into accuracy and control. Calibrate your pen in a stock solution that is the same temperature as your nutrient solution, and has a pH of 7. Place the probes of the meter into the buffer solution and adjust the calibration screw (if necessary) until the needle rests on 7. You can then test the nutrient solution. Several pH pens including the OAKATON do not require adjusting a calibration screw.

Checking the pH

When you measure pH, you want to measure it in both the reservoir and the rockwool because the measurements indicate different things. The pH in the reservoir indicates if the fertilizer has been diluted correctly so it is available to the roots in a soluble form. The pH of the rockwool lets you know the pH level in which the roots are growing. To measure the difference between the pH level in the reservoir and in the rockwool, collect nutrient solution samples from both areas. Use a syringe to extract the sample from the rockwool. Syringes with long nipples and turkey basters with stiff hoses both work well. Because you are concerned most about the pH level in the root zone, be certain to place the syringe at least two inches into the rockwool to extract your solution. Alternatively, if you grow in cubes, you can pick one up and squeeze a small amount of nutrient solution from it.

For consistent test results, take the nutrient solution sample at the same time each day in relation to the irrigation cycle. If you only water once a day, check the rockwool both a couple of hours before and a couple of hours after the irriga-

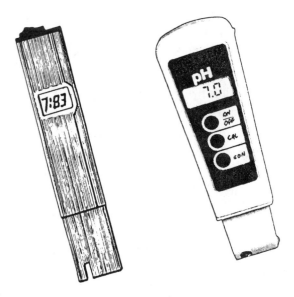

Two pH testing pens.

tion cycle. The readings will show the extreme highs and lows in the pH range. In addition, to preserve accuracy it is important to take each rockwool sample from the same place and in the same manor. It is a good idea to take samples from several different slabs or cubes and mix all of the samples together to get an average after recording all the other readings.

 Rule of Thumb: The pH of the slab and reservoir should range from 5.5 to 6.5.

Place the samples you have taken in clean jars. Measure each sample with the pH meter. The pH of the rockwool should be within one or two tenths of a point of the reservoir solution. It is typical for there to be a slight difference between the pH of the solution in the reservoir and that in the rockwool. Typically the pH of the reservoir is 0.1 to 0.5 lower than the pH of the slab. If you take a sample just before an irrigation cycle, it is likely to show a wider spread between the pH of the input solution and that of the solution in the cube or slab. The pH reading after the irrigation cycle will be closer to the reservoir reading. Although noting a difference in pH between the solution in the reservoir and that in the rockwool is normal, you do not want this difference to fluctuate. If the pH in either location climbs or drops significantly, you need to change the nutrient solution.

Check your pH regularly and record your findings in a notebook or on a calender kept near the garden. You will soon notice patterns developing. If there is a drastic change in the pH, you will know to flush the system or change the nutrient solution.

Your water source, nutrient solution concentration, the geographic location and climate, and even the seasons can all effect pH levels. The carbonate/bicarbonate content or alkalinity of the water measures the resistance of water to acidification. If the carbonate/bicarbonate level is low, little acid is needed to lower pH, and vice versa. Rainy and coastal climates generally have acidic water, while desert regions are prone to alkaline water.

A pH problem may surface in the late autumn, when leaves fall and vegetation is decomposing. The biodegradation process may create an artificially low pH. The acidic leaves lower the pH of the outside soil, and in turn lower the pH of the ground water. This problem is most common in areas serviced by small municipal or well-water. Larger water districts carefully monitor and correct pH, thereby protecting gardeners from potential problems. Be on the lookout for any major environmental changes that could affect the water pH. It is important to keep an eye on the pH at all times.

Correcting pH Imbalances

Recording the findings from your pH tests and noting any shifts spurred by seasons will help you correct pH problems that do arise. If you know that every fall your water becomes acidic, you will be able to correct the imbalance before it ever affects your plants. Generally, gardeners have more problems with overly alkaline solution than they do with acidic solutions. However, there are compounds you can use to raise or lower pH levels.

There are several alkaline compounds you can use to raise pH. Diluted potassium hydroxide is a safe and easy-to-use alternative. Potassium is also a necessary nutrient in balancing pH. Although sodium hydroxide raises pH, it is very caustic. To handle sodium hydroxide, it should be diluted and you *must* wear a mask and gloves. Sodium, although is raises pH, is not a good option because it is toxic to plants and it replaces potassium. That is, when there is an excess of sodium, plants will take up sodium rather than potassium. Sodium hydroxide in concentrated amounts can also severely burn your skin.

 Rule of Thumb: To raise the pH, mix a small amount of diluted potassium hydroxide or potassium bicarbonate per gallon of nutrient solution. Check the pH. Add small amounts of potassium hydroxide or potassium bicarbonate as needed.

Below is a list of substances which will raise pH levels.
Read the list carefully. Not all compounds listed are recommended for garden use.

To raise the pH use:
Hydrated lime - quick to dissolve
Sodium hydroxide (caustic potash) - toxic
Potassium hydroxide - OK - Use *only* in diluted form
Calcium carbonate - insoluble
Baking soda - toxic, contains sodium
Potassium bicarbonate -OK, used in commercial green-
        houses
Potassium phosphate - OK, but will not do much
Dolomite lime - difficult to dissolve
Ground limestone - difficult to dissolve
Calcium chloride - is not recommended but is excel-
        lent for chlorine-loving plants like marsh grasses
        and artichokes.

It is much more common for gardeners to have to
lower the pH of their nutrient solution. Luckily, there are
many ways to do so. Nitric acid works well to control pH, but
it tends to be expensive. Phosphoric acid can cause the calcium to settle out in the bottom of the reservoir. Nitric acid
controls the pH and adds nitrogen. Phosphoric acid, calcium
nitrate, and sulfur compounds also work well to lower pH. If
you use a fertilizer which contains any of these elements, you
must keep a watchful eye on the pH. Vinegar and aspirin will
also lower pH, but their effect dissipates rapidly. You should
only use them as a last resort or in a very small garden. Some
gardeners have success using lemon to lower pH. Simply

pH Up and pH Down are available in both liquid and powder form.

squeeze the juice of fresh lemons into your nutrient solution.

Retail hydroponic stores often sell pH adjusting chemicals in concentrated strengths. Some chemicals are also available in either liquid of powder form. Be very careful when handling concentrated acids or alkalis. They are very caustic and can cause severe skin, eye and lung damage.

 Rule of Thumb: To lower pH, add a small amount of nitric acid or calcium nitrate per gallon of nutrient solution. Mix and recheck.

The following is a list of compounds which lower pH. Read the list carefully to determine what will work most effectively for your garden.

To lower the pH use:
Calcium carbonate - poor choice to alter pH - insoluble
Calcium nitrate - diluted solution is fair
Nitric acid- diluted solution is OK
Phosphoric acid- diluted solution is OK
Phostric acid - diluted solution is OK
Sulfur or sulfuric acid- diluted solution is dangerous
Aspirin- use as a last resort and only in one gallon or less.
Vinegar- use as a last resort and only in one gallon or less.

To determine the amount of chemical you need to alter the pH, first remove a gallon of nutrient solution from the reservoir. Add half as much pH raise or pH lower as is recommended; then check the pH. Wait about 15 minutes, stir, and recheck. Continue to add small amounts of chemical to the solution until you reach the desired pH level. Be sure to keep track of how much you add. Add a proportionate amount of the compound to the balance of the nutrient solution and mix. After altering the pH, check it immediately afterwards, and again the following day. Continue checking the pH on your normal routine to ensure that it remains balanced.

Conditioning

Because new rockwool tends to be alkaline, you need to condition it before planting in it. Conditioning rockwool lowers its pH from around 8.0 to around 5.5. In addition, conditioning improves rockwool by wetting it thoroughly and preventing dry pockets. When new, most brands of rockwool will cause the nutrient solution's pH to rise. The effect is most dramatic with new cubes and slabs, and less pronounced as the rockwool's life continues. To determine the pH of the rockwool, boil a small amount in distilled water. When the water has cooled, measure the pH. If it is above 8.0, soak the rockwool in pH-4.0 phosphoric acid solution for 30 minutes and then flush it out. The phosphoric acid will help to neutralize the alkalinity of most brands of rockwool.

Some growers do not condition their rockwool at all. They include a wetting agent, and a pH balanced fertilizer when soaking the first time. These gardeners report no problem with pH fluctuation.

To condition rockwool, fill the rockwool bag with nutrient solution until the rockwool is fully saturated. The pH of the nutrient solution should be about 4.5 before it soaks into the rockwool. Let the solution sit in the saturated rockwool overnight. After soaking all night, the pH of the nutrient solution in the rockwool should be about 5.5.

 Rule of Thumb: Check the pH regularly to make sure it is between 5.5 and 6.5.

Dissolved Solids and Conductivity Factors

A dissolved solids (DS) measurement indicates how many parts per million (ppm) of dissolved solids exist in a given solution. A reading of 1800 ppm means there are 1800 parts of nutrient in one million parts solution, or 1,800/1,000,000. There are several scales which are used to measure dissolved solids: the dissolved solids scale, the electrical conductivity (EC) scale, and the Conductivity Factor (CF) scale. Of these, the Conductivity Factor scale is most common and useful.

Pure distilled water has no resistance and conducts no electrical current. However, when impurities are added to pure distilled water, it conducts electricity. Your water analysis will indicate the impurities or dissolved solids which exist in your household tap water. These impurities, or elements, conduct electricity when dissolved. For instance, when you add fertilizer to pure water, the Conductivity Factor (CF) climbs.

Conductivity Factor Meters

A simple CF meter works well to measure the overall volume or strength of elements in your water or solution. A digital display in a Conductivity Factor meter measures the amount of current (conductivity) flowing between the two electrodes. A CF reading of "0" indicates there are no solids in the water, or that the water is pure. Pure rainwater has a CF close to 0. If you live in the Midwest or Northeast, check the CF of your rainwater before using it in your garden. The rainwater could be "acid rain." If it is acidic, add small amount of pH raise to the rain to neutralize it, but the other chemicals make it unsuitable to use.. Distilled water purchased at the grocery store may register a small amount of resistance as it is not perfectly pure. Pure water with no resistance is very difficult to obtain.

High quality meters, or "CF pens" have automatic or manual temperature adjustments. Because the CF measurement is sensitive to temperature, these more expensive meters are worth the added cost. If the temperature is not factored into the reading, and inaccurate measurement could be recorded. You must calibrate some CF pens. Calibrating a CF meter is similar to calibrating a pH meter. Simply follow manufacturers instructions. For an accurate reading, make sure your nutrient solution and stock solution are the same temperature. Expect your meter

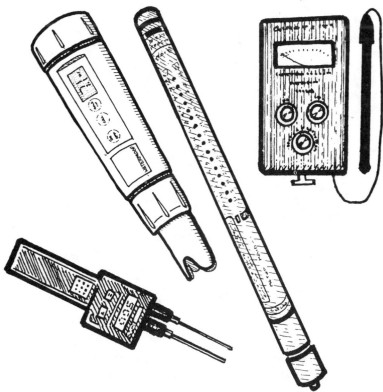

Several different CF meters.

to last at least a year. Many meters last five years or longer if well taken care of. Read all the instructions thoroughly on care and maintenance. . Watch for corrosion build-up on the probes of your meter. When the probes are corroded, you will not get an accurate reading.

Although a CF meter can measure the amount of conductivity in a solution, it can not delineate nutrients. For example, a CF reading of 1.0 could mean there are sodium and sulfur in a solution. On the other hand, a CF of 1.0 could also measure a complete and balanced solution which contains all necessary nutrients in the proper proportions.

CF is only a valid measurement when you start with the proper ratio of nutrients in your solution.

 Rule of Thumb: Check the CF of your water, slab, and runoff regularly.

Checking the Conductivity Factor

To check the CF, collect nutrient solution samples from both the reservoir and the rockwool. To save time and effort, collect CF and pH samples simultaneously. Use the same guidelines for each collection. That is, use a syringe or baster and collect a sample from at least two inches deep in the rockwool. At the same time, collect a sample from the reservoir.

Place each sample in a clean jar. Use a CF meter to measure the samples. Under normal conditions, the CF in the slab should be a bit higher than the nutrient solution in the reservoir. If the CF in the rockwool is substantially higher than that in the reservoir, you have a salt buildup in the rockwool. To correct this imbalance, flush the rockwool thoroughly with diluted nutrient solution and replenish or change the nutrient solution.

CF Imbalances

Many factors can alter the CF balance in your garden. If your garden is under-watered or dried out, the CF reading will rise. In fact, the CF may increase to two or three times as high as the input solution when too little water is applied to the rockwool. This increase in slab CF causes some nutrients to build up faster than others. For example, when the CF doubles, the amount of sodium increases four to six fold!

NOTE: There should not be any sodium present in your garden unless it is in the water supply.

To easily control the Conductivity Factor content of the nutrient solution, let 10 to 20 percent of the solution "run-off" to waste after each watering. This run-off will carry away any excess salt build-up. Catch this "waste" nutrient solution to use in your outdoor garden. If the CF level in your rockwool solution is too high, increase the amount of run-off you create with each flush. For example, instead of a 10-20 percent run-off, flush so 20-30 percent of the solution runs off. To raise the CF, add more fertilizer to the solution or change the nutrient solution.

Greenlite Hydroponics near Melbourne, Australia put together the following information to explain the difference between parts per million (PPM) and Conductivity Factor (CF). The information is so good, we are printing it exactly as it appears in their brochure.

A nutrient tester's main function is to measure Electrical Conductivity (EC), in solution. EC is the ability of a solution to carry an electrical current. Dissolved Ionic Salts create electrical current in solution, the main constituent of hydroponic solutions is ionic salts.

EC s commonly measured in either (a) Millisiemans per Centimeter (MS/CM) or (b) Microsiemens per Centimeter (US/CM).

One Microsiemen/CM = 1000 Millisiemens/CM

So where does parts per million come in??

Most of our customers seem to be unaware that their PPM testers actually measure in EC but then show a conversion reading in PPM. This may seem adequate, but unfortunately the two scales (EC and PPM) are not directly related. The reason being that each type or salt gives a different electronic discharge reading. A standard is selected which assumes "so much EC means so much salt". Or in our case - nutrient in the solution. The result is only a rough idea of the current PPM within your nutrient solution, a ball park figure - a very wide ball park figure!!!

To complicate matters further, currently within the hydroponic industry, nutrient tester manufacturers use different standards to convert to the PPM reading.

1. Hanna   1MS/CM = 500 PPM
2. Eutech   1MS/CM = 640 PPM
3. New Zealand Hydro. 1MS/CM = 700 PPM

As you can see advice given in PPM may be confusing, but don't be too concerned as we are providing an easy reference chart with the conversions listed. Then you can run your nutrient at the same level regardless of the meter purchased. You will see by the scale of the PPM reading you obtain from your meter can gave quite drastic differences depending on which brand of meter you use.

May we recommend using a CF as a nutrient scale???

1. CF has a direct relationship scale wise to EC, preventing any discrepancy in conversion i.e. 1 MS/CM = 10 CF e.g. 0.7 EC = 7 CF.

Conversion scale from ppm/CF.

EC MS/CM	Hanna	Eutech	Truncheon	CF
0.5		0.64	0.70	0
0.1	50 ppm	64 ppm	70 ppm	1
0.2	100 ppm	128 ppm	140 ppm	2
0.3	150 ppm	192 ppm	210 ppm	3
0.4	200 ppm	256 ppm	280 ppm	4
0.5	250 ppm	320 ppm	350 ppm	5
0.6	300 ppm	384 ppm	420 ppm	6
0.7	350 ppm	448 ppm	490 ppm	7
0.8	400 ppm	512 ppm	560 ppm	8
0.9	450 ppm	576 ppm	630 ppm	9
1.0	500 ppm	640 ppm	700 ppm	10
1.1	550 ppm	704 ppm	770 ppm	11
1.2	600 ppm	768 ppm	840 ppm	12
1.3	650 ppm	832 ppm	910 ppm	13
1.4	700 ppm	896 ppm	980 ppm	14
1.5	750 ppm	960 ppm	1050 ppm	15
1.6	800 ppm	1024 ppm	1120 ppm	16
1.7	850 ppm	1088 ppm	1190 ppm	17
1.8	900 ppm	1152 ppm	1260 ppm	18
1.9	950 ppm	1260 ppm	1330 ppm	19
2.0	1000 ppm	1280 ppm	1400 ppm	20
2.1	1050 ppm	1344 ppm	1470 ppm	21
2.2	1100 ppm	1408 ppm	1540 ppm	22
2.3	1150 ppm	1472 ppm	1610 ppm	23
2.4	1200 ppm	1536 ppm	1680 ppm	24
2.5	1250 ppm	1600 ppm	1750 ppm	25
2.6	1300 ppm	1664 ppm	1820 ppm	26
2.7	1350 ppm	1728 ppm	1890 ppm	27
2.8	1400 ppm	1792 ppm	1960 ppm	28
2.9	1450 ppm	1856 ppm	2030 ppm	29
3.0	1500 ppm	1920 ppm	2100 ppm	30
3.1	1550 ppm	1984 ppm	2170 ppm	.1
3.2	1600 ppm	2048 ppm	2240 ppm	32

2. CF uses simple to use 0 to 100 scale "0" representing zero ionic activity - if no dissolved salts.

3. Throughout the hydroponic industry the CF scale does not alter, preventing different interpretations of nutrient values.

4. Most hydroponic publications advise in CF.

5. Why should we bother converting to PPM, it has no advantages and only leads to inaccuracy.

Chapter Six
Rockwool Gardens &
Growing Tips

In the preceding chapters, you learned about the many attributes of using rockwool in your indoor garden. You learned how to care for it, how to plant in it, how to irrigate it, and how to use it as a vessel to supply nutrients to your plants. In this chapter, we will expand on the knowledge you have gained thus far, and integrate many of the considerations which we have discussed separately in previous chapters. To do this, we will use examples of several hypothetical rockwool gardens: several kinds of cube gardens and a slab garden.

By focusing on specific gardens, you will be able to understand how your equipment, the nutrient solution, pH balance, CF level, and irrigation cycle work with the rockwool to provide an optimum environment for a successful high performance garden. Remember, these are only examples intended to give you a complete picture or how a particular rockwool garden works. There are an infinite number of ways to set up rockwool gardens. Depending on your space, environment, and crop choice, you will want to modify these examples to best suit your needs.

A Cube Garden

One of rockwool's greatest assets is the ease with which it can be used in plant propagation. Plant propagation refers to the methods gardeners use to increase their plant stock. There are two basic kinds of plant propagation: sexual and a-sexual. Growing plants from seed is a form of sexual reproduction, while rooting cuttings is a form of a-sexual propagation. Rockwool can be used successfully with either. In fact, many gardeners use rockwool cubes to start seedlings, root cuttings, and grow small plants.

Rockwool cubes out-perform soil media for propagation for numerous reasons. Rockwool cubes are a better value than peat pellets or rockwool starter cubes. They are half the price, easier to use, and more forgiving. Rockwool cubes are neater and easier to transport than propagation trays filled with soil. Because they are so neat and easy to handle, transplanting cuttings or seedlings grown in rockwool is virtually effortless. In addition, because rockwool has no nutrients of its own, gardeners can have complete control over the nutrients their delicate seedlings and cuttings receive. Cubes can be watered by hand from above the plant, or flooded from below. In fact, cubes even work to wick nutrient solution up to plants. In this section you will find a discussion of the many of attributes and uses for, rockwool cubes. In addition to presenting information on how to create your own cube garden, we provide easy-to-follow guidelines for growing healthy plants in rockwool cubes.

Although this cube garden example relies on a flood and drain system, you can employ a variety of different hydro-

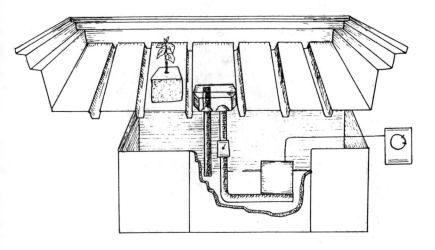

This large ebb and flow table has short sides and deep groves to channel nutrient solution back to the drain.

ponic systems in rockwool cube gardens. Remember, our examples are intended as guidelines only. You can alter and elaborate on the systems we describe to fit your needs.

You can create a cube garden growing bed of almost any size or shape. The only stringent criteria is that it be able to hold water. Because the cubes need to be submerged for flushing on a weekly or bi-weekly basis, the growing table should be slightly deeper than the cubes. For three inch cubes, look for a growing bed or table with four-inch sides and large, flat ridges along the bottom for drainage. Although a deep table is recommended, many gardeners maintain that complete submersion is not necessary when gardening with cubes. They are able to grow healthy gardens using growing beds with only two-inch sides.

Healthy roots are growing out the bottom of a cube.

The most critical area to control in a rockwool cube garden is the root zone. Proper drainage is essential to plant health. Although you want to keep roots evenly moist, you do not want them to sit in stagnant water. Puddles of stagnant water promote root rot and fungus growth. To avoid such problems, water must drain freely. When building or purchasing a table, make sure that it drains completely when it is level, or at a slight incline. If puddling water becomes a problem, set your cubes on a shallow grate above the water. If you use an inclined table, be aware that rockwool shifts into the lowest point of the growing bed and will become waterlogged unless there is a drain outlet below the rockwool. Low spots create soggy conditions and promote rot and fungus growth. Ideally, a high performance growing table will have a bottom with broad ridges

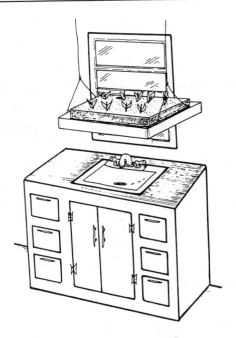

Window sill garden using 1020 nursery flat.

which allow the rockwool to lay flat. It should also have narrow gutters to carry away runoff.

Another way to enhance drainage is to place perlite under your rockwool blocks. Because perlite is so light, you may find that it floats to one end of the table, and perhaps gets washed down the drain. Both washed gravel and, expanded clay (leca) work well to create airspace below the cubes but be careful with LIGHTWEIGHT expanded clay because it may wash away.

Window Sill Gardens

In this section you will find a comparison of two easy-to-use window sill cube gardens, neither of which employ a

drain. We'll start seedlings in one garden, and grow fresh
kitchen herbs in the other. We will provide you with detailed
instructions on how to create both. Creating a window sill garden is easy and inexpensive. In fact, you can make a window
sill seed propagation garden from two 1020 nursery flats (a
1020 flat measures 10 inches by 20 inches) and a turkey baster.

For spring seedlings or cuttings use a mesh bottomed
flat as a garden bed. Set it inside a solid bottomed, watertight
1020 nursery flat. The solid bottomed flat serves as a reservoir.
Place the rockwool cubes in the mesh bottomed flat. This garden is similar to the soil seed starter kits available at many retail
nurseries and mail order stores. However, this rockwool starter
kit is easier and more productive than its soil counterpart.
Once you try it, you will love it.

Use a turkey baster to draw nutrient solution for the
bottom flat. Apply this solution to the top of the rockwool
cubes. Mix the nutrient solution to between a quarter and a
half of the recommended strength. Depending on your local
climate, and the size of your plants, you will need to irrigate
once or twice weekly. For example, because seedling have larger root systems than cuttings, they will need more nutrient
solution. Keep your rockwool cubes wet, while also retaining
good drainage. Within a few weeks, the roots will grow out the
bottom of the rockwool and into the nutrient solution. When
the roots show through the cubes, harden-off by placing the
garden outdoors in the shade for a couple of hours for several
days. Hardening-off before transplanting will ensure plant vital-
ity.

The second window sill cube garden example has a
larger reservoir and takes up a little more space. To make this
garden, use a flexible hose to attach a reservoir bucket to a garden bed made from a nursery flat. Drill a half-inch hole in
both the bucket and the garden bed. Insert a threaded half-

Transplanting a small cube into a pre-drilled hole. Rockwool cubes and slabs are designed to make transplanting very easy.

inch male PVC fitting with a rubber washer through the hole. Screw a threaded, half-inch female PVC fitting with a washer onto the male fitting. Then glue a two-foot piece of one-inch garden hose inside the female fitting. To irrigate, raise the reservoir bucket above the garden bed so that the nutrient solution flows into the bed. Lower the bucket after the cubes have been flooded (about 5 minutes) to let the solution drain back into the bucket. Once set up, this garden creates no mess or fuss. Just lift and lower the bucket once or twice daily. Change the nutrient solution weekly.

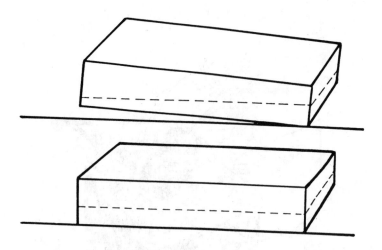

Elevate one end of the slab so the run-off flows back to the reservoir. Set the slabs at a two percent slope,

Slab Gardens

Although cube gardens are ideal for cuttings, seedling, and small plants, they are not ideal for large plants. When your seedlings or cuttings grow too big for a small cube garden, you will want to employ a larger slab garden. Once you see roots coming out of the sides of your cube garden, you know it is time to transplant to a slab garden. To transplant cubes into a slab, cut holes the same size as the cubes in the top of the rockwool bag. Then simply set the cubes into the hole in slab.

Rockwool slabs are designed for greenhouse flower and vegetable production. However, they can also be used successfully in kitchen or patio gardens. Rockwool slabs outperform their soil counterparts because they hold nutrient solution longer. Rockwool slabs promote lush, healthy growth.

To make a simple slab garden, place a six or eight-inch

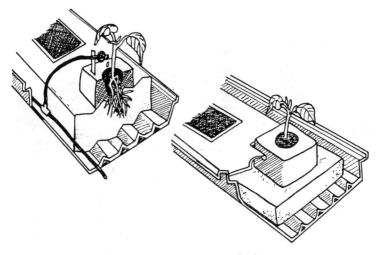

These small growing beds have grooves on the bottom to carry nutri-ent solution back to the reservoir.

by three-inch by three-foot slab in a garden bed with good drainage. Slabs perform best in areas that provide consistent drainage such as a concrete floor, patio, or greenhouse. If you do not have a garden bed, you can use plastic sleeves instead. Once the plastic sleeves are placed around the slabs, they form their own garden bed. These sleeves are important for strong plants. When the roots grow out of the sides of the slabs, they grow into the moist environment between the rockwool and the plastic. This space forms an ideal growing environment. Place a plastic grate under the slab to improve drainage. Once the slab is set in place, soak it thoroughly.

To make use of gravity, elevate one end of the slab so the run-off flows back to the reservoir. Set the slabs at a two percent slope, which is equivalent to a drop of about a half inch from one end of a 36-inch slab to the other. Even if you can not rest your slabs on a slope, you can still make use of

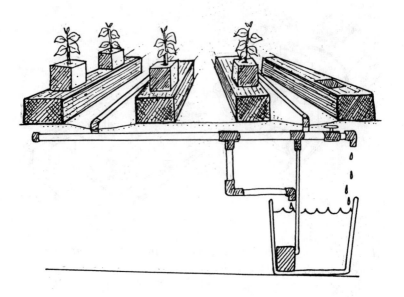

A small slab garden ready to be planted.

gravity to deliver the nutrient solution to the reservoir. Drip
tubing will help carry run-off for slabs that are set at ground
level.

　　Once you have your slabs arranged in an appropriate
floor plan (for instance, side by side, or around the perimeter of
a deck or patio), you may need to cut drainage slits in the sides
and bottoms of your slabs. You will need between two and six
drainage slits on each slab. After the drainage slits have been
cut, slip the uncovered wet slabs into plastic sleeves, or set then
into a garden bed. Make sure there is enough sleeving at the
end to channel drainage. Seal the other end of the bag with
duct tape, or fold it shut and secure it closed with clothes pins.
The sleeving must be dry before you seal it with tape. If sleeving is unavailable, cover the exposed slabs with two-ply plastic.

Place the black side on the inside to stop algae growth, and the white on the outside to reflect light. We also recommend that you place a drip emitter next to the plant stem to apply water. When you irrigate from the top and the water runs through the rockwool, the surface does not stay wet, and algae does not grow.

Once you have planted your slab garden, take care to maintain optimum climactic conditions for your plants. You will need to control heat, light, moisture, pH, and CF. Follow the guidelines discussed throughout this book, and refer to the "Growing Tips" section below for further details.

Re-using Slabs

Rockwool can be re-used. Although re-using your slabs makes gardening more economical, re-used slabs are more prone to disease and other problems than are new rockwool slabs. We advise that you do not reuse rockwool slabs. Old roots that are nearly impossible to remove attract bacteria and fungi if the slabs are not totally sterilized. Most gardeners prefer not to take the chance of having any problems.

To re-use rockwool slabs, remove and discard any cubes you have transplanted. Remove the slab from the plastic sleeving. When all the plastic is removed, set the slabs on end and blow them dry with a fan. Scrape off any old dry roots from the sides and bottom of the slabs.

If you are concerned about virus, fungus, or disease, discard the slabs or steam sterilize them. A wallpaper steamer works to sterilize slabs because it can raise the temperature to 212 degrees Fahrenheit (100 degrees Celsius). In order to kill all the insects, nematodes, fungi, bacteria, and viruses, it is important to make sure that the entire slab is steamed for a minimum of thirty minutes.

After the slab dries out, it is ready to be reused. Turn the slab over, bottom side up, and insert it into a clean sleeve or set into a clean bed. After you condition the slabs, you can replant in them.

Growing Tips

In this section, you will find a series of suggestions which will help improve the quality and yield of your rockwool garden.

By using rockwool cubes, you can plant your cuttings and seedlings closely together, and still encourage a healthy yield. Because rockwool cubes are square, they pack together more closely than do round pots, providing 20 percent more root growing area. Although they are packed tightly together, plants can be kept short enough so that light penetrates to the bottom leaves. Plants grown in this manner grow so fast, there is no time for lower leaves to yellow. In addition, the crop grows fast and strong before insects can cause damage. Because the roots are somewhat confined, flowering plants are forced to flower a few days sooner than they otherwise would. The plants are packed so closely together that they support, but do not suffocate, one another. Staking is unnecessary.

If you are rooting cuttings, you must take many cuttings every several weeks. Pay attention to how long it takes for your cuttings to root. You do not want them to become root-bound.

Start seeds and cuttings in one-inch rockwool cubes. While small seeds can be laid on top of the rockwool and then gently pushed into the medium, larger seeds must be inserted into pre-drilled holes. Because the rockwool is the moisture

Transplanting a small rockwool cube into soil.

and nutrient carrying medium in your garden, the seeds must be in constant contact with it to grow successfully. Push rockwool over the hole so that the seed stays in contact with the rockwool. When roots emerge from the bottom and the sides of the cubes, transplant into pre-drilled three-inch or larger cubes. To harden-off, set the entire flat in the shade outdoors for several hours each day. Then leave the garden outdoors in a cold frame or greenhouse all night when the last chance of frost is past. Transplant the rockwool cubes into the garden after they have been hardened off for several days.

 Rule of Thumb: The first sign of root rot (pythium) is brown roots. In the final stage, the stem turns brown inside and the plant dies..

When growing small seedlings and young cuttings, use a mild nutrient solution (quarter to half strength). Tender plants can not endure a heavy nutrient concentration. Saturate one-inch rockwool cubes with half strength nutrient solution. Increase fertilizer to full strength after you transplant them. Set three-inch cubes in the garden bed, and saturate with half strength nutrient solution until they are established.

Remember, the nutrient solution performs best at 70-75 degrees F (22-24 degrees C), but will function well down to 50 degrees F. Use an aquarium heater to maintain this temperature range in the reservoir.

Although rockwool cubes are durable, the roots they contain are frail. To avoid damaging the delicate root system, be gentle and patient while you are transplanting. You can cause transplant shock if roots are broken off and not gently returned to the medium. When you plan to transplant into soil, it is best to propagate in one-inch unwrapped cubes. Rockwool and soil each have their own distinct composition, and each holds water at a different rate. Because soil is drier than rockwool, it attracts the water held in rockwool and thereby dries the rockwool out. If you keep the soil moist, you can avoid the danger of water loss from the rockwool. The larger the cube, the more difficult transplanting will be due to this change in surface tension. However, if large clusters of roots dangle from the bottom of a four-inch cube, you will probably be able to transplant it without a problem. Remember to remove the plastic sleeve from around the rockwool before transplanting into soil. After carefully transplanting your cuttings or seedlings, cycle nutrient solution through the garden so the roots get saturated.

Rockwool remains wet enough that damping-off (rotting where the stem and soil meet) can become a serious problem. To avoid problems with damping-off or fungus growth, let

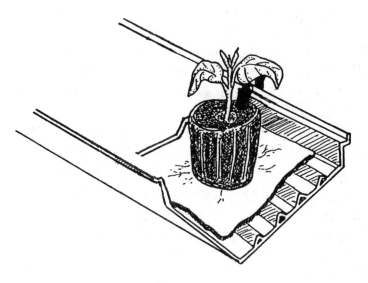

Net pot full of rockwool for NFT (Nutrient Film Technique) hydroponic system.

the surface of the rockwool dry out between waterings.

When you water, over-water by 10-30 percent to encourage flooding. This will help wash away diluted nutrients and toxic mineral build-ups. Even if you over-water by 20 to 30 percent, a build-up of elements might occur. By flooding rockwool cubes completely once a week, you will be able to retain a healthy ion balance.

Setting your cubes in a lattice bottomed nursery flat promotes circulation of oxygen below the roots. Just after the nutrient solution drains back into the reservoir, look for air bubbles on the bottom of the rockwool garden bed, between the cubes and the bottom. If you pick up a cube, you should also be able to see air bubbles attached to the lattice below. These tiny air bubbles burst periodically and release oxygen, thereby forming a perfect climate for nutrient uptake.

If nematodes (microscopic worms that can live in rockwool), become a problem, apply *Bacillus thuringiensis* (*Bt/H-14*) sold under the brand names Vectobac and Gnatrol. *Bt/H-14* is the absolute best nematode control available. for more information on *Bt/H-14* see the *New Revised Gardening Indoors* by George F. Van Patten.

Remember, growing a healthy rockwool garden is primarily a matter of controlling all the factors that affect plant growth, including pH, light, air, water, nutrients, and the growing medium. If you do, your garden will reap excellent yields. Because regular monitoring and maintenance of the pH and CF are necessary for vigorous plant growth, it is important to use reliable measuring devices. pH and CF pens are easy to use and economical.

Artificial light, provided by a 400 watt metal halide light, attached to a timer, makes total climate control possible. By using grow lights, your garden will be predicable and easier to control than an outdoor garden. And the increase in your electric bill is minimal. For delicate cuttings and seedlings, do not provide in excess of 500 foot-candles of light. To induce vegetative growth, keep the light intensity at a minimum of 1000 foot-candles for 18 hours a day. To stimulate flowering in short day plants such as chrysanthemums and Christmas cactus, increase the light intensity at 2500 foot-candles, but decrease the photoperiod to 12 hours a day. If you use natural light, choose non-daylight (photoperiod) sensitive plants. For more information on gardening with HID lights, see *Gardening Indoors with HID Lights* by George F. Van Patten and Alyssa F. Bust.

Drain and clean your garden every 2 or 3 months. Use a mild bleach solution and a sponge to remove any built up algae, slime, or sediments from the growing beds and holding tank.

Index

Gardening Indoors with CO₂

96 pages - illustrated - 5 1/2" x 8 1/2" - **$12.95**
Packed with the latest information about carbon dioxide enrichment -
how to get the most out of CO_2 generators and emitters available
today. Easy step-by-step instructions on setting up CO_2 in your garden room. Double your harvest with CO_2 .

Gardening Indoors with Cuttings

96 pages - illustrated - 5 1/2" x 8 1/2" - **$12.95**
Growing cuttings is fun and easy. This book is loaded with the most
productive methods and information. Take cuttings to control plant
growth and achieve super yields. Easy step-by-step instructions teach
beginners and experts alike how-to take perfect cuttings.

Gardening Indoors with HID Lights

160 pages - illustrated - 5 1/2" x 8 1/2" - **$14.95**
This book is the definitive book on high intensity discharge (HID)
lighting and plant growth. This book overflows with the latest information on high-tech lights. If you use HIDs, you must have this book.

Gardening Indoors with Rockwool

128 pages - illustrated - 5 1/2" x 8 1/2" - **$14.95**
New and updated volume of *Gardening: The Rockwool Book*. It is reformatted and packed with the latest information on rockwool.

Gardening Indoors with CO_2

96 pages - illustrated - 5 1/2" x 8 1/2" - **$12.95**
Packed with the latest information about carbon dioxide enrichment - how to get the most out of CO_2 generators and emitters available today. Easy step-by-step instructions on setting up CO_2 in your garden room. Double your harvest with CO_2 .

Gardening Indoors with Cuttings

96 pages - illustrated - 5 1/2" x 8 1/2" - **$12.95**
Growing cuttings is fun and easy. This book is loaded with the most productive methods and information. Take cuttings to control plant growth and achieve super yields. Easy step-by-step instructions teach beginners and experts alike how-to take perfect cuttings.

Gardening Indoors with HID Lights

160 pages - illustrated - 5 1/2" x 8 1/2" - **$14.95**
This book is the definitive book on high intensity discharge (HID) lighting and plant growth. This book overflows with the latest information on high-tech lights. If you use HIDs, you must have this book.

Gardening Indoors with Rockwool

128 pages - illustrated - 5 1/2" x 8 1/2" - **$14.95**
New and updated volume of *Gardening: The Rockwool Book*. It is reformatted and packed with the latest information on rockwool.

New Revised Gardening Indoors	**$19.95**	*Shipping, handling & insurance $3 per book*
Gardening Indoors With Rockwool	**$14.95**	
Gardening Indoors With Cuttings	**$12.95**	
Gardening Indoors With HID Lights	**$14.95**	*Call for shipping costs for more than 2 books.*
Gardening Indoors With CO_2	**$12.95**	
Shipping, handling & insurance (per book)	**$3.00**	

Ship to: _____

Address _____

City _____ State _____ Zip _____

Telephone _____

Checks & Money Orders only

Wholesale Clients Wanted

Orders (510) 236-3360
Van Patten Publishing
38912 NE Borin Road, Washougal, WA 98671-9527

Gardening Indoors with CO_2

96 pages - illustrated - 5 1/2" x 8 1/2" - **$12.95**

Packed with the latest information about carbon dioxide enrichment - how to get the most out of CO_2 generators and emitters available today. Easy step-by-step instructions on setting up CO_2 in your garden room. Double your harvest with CO_2 .

Gardening Indoors with Cuttings

96 pages - illustrated - 5 1/2" x 8 1/2" - **$12.95**

Growing cuttings is fun and easy. This book is loaded with the most productive methods and information. Take cuttings to control plant growth and achieve super yields. Easy step-by-step instructions teach beginners and experts alike how-to take perfect cuttings.

Gardening Indoors with HID Lights

160 pages - illustrated - 5 1/2" x 8 1/2" - **$14.95**

This book is the definitive book on high intensity discharge (HID) lighting and plant growth. This book overflows with the latest information on high-tech lights. If you use HIDs, you must have this book.

Gardening Indoors with Rockwool

128 pages - illustrated - 5 1/2" x 8 1/2" - **$14.95**

New and updated volume of *Gardening: The Rockwool Book*. It is reformatted and packed with the latest information on rockwool.

New Revised Gardening Indoors	**$19.95**	*Shipping, handling & insurance $3 per book*
Gardening Indoors With Rockwool	**$14.95**	
Gardening Indoors With Cuttings	**$12.95**	
Gardening Indoors With HID Lights	**$14.95**	*Call for shipping costs for more than 2 books.*
Gardening Indoors With CO_2	**$12.95**	
Shipping, handling & insurance (per book) **$3.00**		

Ship to: _____

Address _____

City _____ State _____ Zip _____

Telephone _____

Checks & Money Orders only

Wholesale Clients Wanted

Orders (510) 236-3360

Van Patten Publishing

38912 NE Borin Road, Washougal, WA 98671-9527